Social Media Marketing

Unlock the Secrets of Personal Branding to Grow Your Small Business and Become an Influencer Using YouTube, Facebook, Instagram, Blogging for SEO, Twitter, and Advertising

Contents

Introduction

Social media is a rapidly growing ecosystem that has developed as a strong platform for small businesses and influencers to make their impact on the world. Thanks to social media, individuals who were once stuck working for corporations or other business owners now have the opportunity to choose to go into business for themselves. There are many reasons as to why someone might want to go into business for themselves, ranging from developing a secondary income to support their lifestyle to becoming complete digital nomads. Regardless of what has attracted you to building a presence online, getting involved in social media marketing is a powerful way to leverage the internet to help you build a successful business.

In *Social Media Marketing,* you are going to discover how you can carve out your unique path in the online space and turn that into your marketing system so that you can develop your business online! It is important that as you read through this book, you follow it in order to ensure that you are developing a well-designed foundation for yourself to grow on. The more consistent you are with how you develop your brand and market yourself from day one, the further you are going to get in the online space.

As you will learn throughout this book, consistency is key. In addition to consistency, you need to have uniqueness or something that sets you apart from the rest of the people who are trying to generate the same buzz that you are. As you apply your consistency and uniqueness to your business and marketing strategies, you will discover that developing your name in the online space is not as challenging as it may seem. In fact, creating a clear-cut path and using that path to generate success can be extremely easy!

If you are ready to identify your vision, carve out your unique brand, and market yourself online so that you can earn an additional side income or become a full-blown digital nomad, now is the time! Enjoy reading this book, and take your time so that you can truly develop consistency for yourself and your brand!

Chapter 1: Creating Your Vision

Before you can begin creating anything, no matter what that is, you need to have a vision of what it is that you are setting out to create. To help you get really clear about what it is that you want to develop in the online space, and how you want your legacy to look, we are going to discover how you can create and clarify your vision for your online brand. Creating a vision is about dreaming without limits, permitting yourself to think large, and then fine-tuning your idea so that it serves what you desire to gain from life. The best part about creating your vision for your business is that you are not required to dream small in any way whatsoever. You can dream up as large of a vision as you desire, and there is nothing to say that you cannot make that vision come true, so long as you are willing to put in the work to get there. In this chapter, you will develop a vision that will not only give you something to work toward, but that will also spark excitement in you so that you are eager to rise and work toward your vision every single day.

First Things First: What is A Personal Brand?

A personal brand is a form of a brand that is developed around a single individual. When someone decides to personally brand, they take their name or their alias and turn it into their "brand name". In other words, this is who and what they become known for. For example, Oprah is a woman, but she is also a personal brand as anytime you think of Oprah you likely think of an afternoon talk show, a magazine, and an inspirational and motivational speaker. Developing a personal brand essentially requires you to decide that you want to go into business for yourself and that you want to be the business. You are going to be the face of the company, the individual providing whatever services it is that you may provide, and the commodity that is being marketed.

Personal branding requires you to know what it is that you are creating, and what it is that you are offering to your audience. There are many types of personal brands that exist, and later in this very chapter, you are going to discover what it is that you want to create for your personal brand. In the meantime, to give you an idea of what is available to you, you could consider personal branding as anything from an influencer to a coach or even an artist. Essentially, any skill you have that you want to offer to your audience can be turned into your offer, and you become the brand or the entity associated with the offer that you have available. Through doing this, you become known for your creations, and you give yourself the perfect platform to sell your creations or services to a well-curated audience of people who are actually interested in what you have to offer.

Common Challenges People Face with Personal Brands

Personal brands are one of the most fascinating styles of brands to develop, and they can also be one of the more challenging types of brands to develop. Personal brands can be more challenging because they are entirely built on you as a person, which means that you are going to be turning yourself into a public image and promoting yourself. Most people find this to be challenging for two reasons: first, it changes the way your privacy works, and second is that it does require you to grow as a person. Privacy-wise, developing a personal brand will require you to be willing to share yourself with the world. Although you can still keep parts of your life private, certain things will inevitably need to be shared so that you can develop an image that is interesting enough for people to follow. It is important that you become very clear from day one what it is that you are willing to share, and what parts of your life you want to keep private to refrain from being too open with your audience.

Many newer personal brands may feel like it is a fun idea to share everything with their audience, but they do not realize that this can come with many backlashes. People who share too much open themselves up in many vulnerable ways, which can lead to a lot of troubles if you have anything personal going on in your life. If you do ever find that you have something you want to keep to yourself, keeping it private will be more challenging if your audience is used to you giving them everything all of the time. For that reason, it is imperative that a personal brand knows exactly what they are and what they are not willing to share with their audience. This simple little tool of deciding what will be public and what will be private can support you in avoiding many troubles and frustrations later on down the line. It will also help you provide a cleaner and more focused image to your audience when you share online.

The second difficulty that some people face is how much growth can be demanded of you when you are a personal brand. People are often unaware of how much energy and effort it can take to show up for your audience every day and provide parts of your personal self to the world so that your brand can continue developing. You will need to learn how to manage your emotions, balance your life so that you can offer parts of yourself to your audience without draining yourself, and how to stay in a state of healthy growth so that your growth truly benefits you in the long run. This challenge can easily be overcome by remaining committed to staying curious about how you can continue growing so long as you choose to be in business as a personal brand.

These two common difficulties that people face when they begin personally branding themselves can be overcome with the awareness of their existence and the willingness to grow past them. So long as you remain aware of how they may arise in your life, you can always develop a personal brand that will be incredibly strong. Simply be willing to identify how you can continue strengthening it and reinforcing it, and you will be developing a brand that serves you, and that continues to grow over time.

Identifying What Your Personal Brand Is

Now that you have an idea of what a personal brand is and how you can develop one that will remain sustainable, it is time for you to begin identifying what your personal brand is! For this section, we are not going to be focusing on your persona so much as your actual niche. Before you can decide whom you are going to be for your audience, you need to decide what it is that you are offering your audience and how you can offer it in a way that fits their needs. Developing your niche comes in three phases: deciding what industry you want to be in, picking a part of that industry that you want to fit into, and then deciding whom you are targeting with your brand.

Deciding what industry you are going to be a part of should be relatively simple—the chances are that you already have a strong idea of what it is that you want to do. You may have been watching other personal brands or influencers in the online space for some time now, which may be why you realize that this option is available for you too. If this is the case, stick to the first industry that comes to mind when you read this as you can pretty well guarantee that this is going to be the best industry for you to be a part of. It is likely that this is the one that you are most passionate about and that you are going to have the most fun developing in this industry, so ideally this is the industry that you should go with. If you have any doubts around this industry, such as whether or not you have enough skills for it or if you are qualified enough to be a part of it, consider the fact that skills can easily be developed over time. The key here is to pick an industry that you are going to be able to remain passionate about for a long time so that you develop a sustainable brand, not just in general but for you as a person.

If you are not yet sure what industry you want to be a part of, or if you cannot decide between a few different industries of interest, there are a few different ways that you can decide. Choosing an industry comes down to three things: what interests you, what fits with your lifestyle, and what offers you the future that you want. You want to choose an industry that is going to spark your interest so that you can remain focused on it and continue developing in it. People who are a part of industries that they are not interested in, or that they do not have a large interest in, often find themselves bored and uninterested in pursuing their businesses because they do not truly care about what they are doing. You need to pick an industry that is going to excite you to wake up and work every morning; otherwise, you are not going to want to do any work at all.

You also need to choose an industry that fits your lifestyle so that it is easy for you to incorporate the work into what you are already doing. Especially early on, being able to be a part of an industry that is relevant to your life is essential so that you can work it into your existing schedule. Then, over time, this part of your life can grow as you can generate more consistent income through your personal brand so you can begin stepping away from any other career obligations that you may not like as much. So, if you are naturally very busy and find that you are not particularly drawn to spending time at the gym or cooking healthy foods, starting your career as a fitness coach or a health guru just because it is a popular industry is not ideal. If you find that amidst your busy lifestyle you find joy in learning how to dress fashionably and look great even on a time crunch, then maybe launching a fashion blog would be ideal for you. Essentially, you need something that is going to fit into your lifestyle.

Lastly, you want to be a part of an industry that is going to offer you the future that you want so you have something fun to work toward. Think about what you truly want for yourself and your life, and then begin defining what type of industry would fit into that. For example, maybe you want a fast-paced growth-oriented lifestyle where you can regularly be taking action on personal development. In that case, you may find more joy in being a marketer or a life coach than you would in being a product tester, as the world of marketing is more fast-paced and growth-oriented, whereas product testing will always be relatively the same. If you are more into routine and doing things the same, then you may prefer to become someone who develops tutorial videos or reviews videos for your industry, rather than someone who is always traveling around the world offering reviews of various exotic locations. Finding out what works with your bigger picture is an important step in ensuring that your business actually fits your overall vision.

Clarifying Your Personal Brand's Focus

Once you have identified what your industry will be, it is time for you to start getting clearer on what your focus is going to be on. Here, you want to laser focus as much as you possibly can to ensure that you have a very clear intention for what it is that you are offering your audience. You want to get clear not only on *what* area you are serving but *how* when it comes to clarifying your personal brand's focus.

The first step here is choosing one segment of your niche that you want to serve so that you know what it is you are offering to your audience. For example, say you want to get into the makeup industry, perhaps by being a beauty influencer. Your next step, then, would be to identify what makeup services you are offering to your audience so that you can offer something clear and consistent. Perhaps you would want to offer drugstore beauty tutorials for makeup lovers on a budget, or high-end makeup product reviews for those who shop for luxurious brands like Tom Ford and Chanel makeup. Alternatively, you may want to offer makeup tutorials for males, or even costume makeup tutorials. You need to decide what specific area you want to serve so that you know what focus you need to take in your business.

To help you get clear on what your brand is offering, consider how it is that you want to offer your services and whom you want to offer them to. Get clear on what audience you are hoping to serve, and start brainstorming what ways you could serve them that would fit in with what vision it is that you desire to create. The more clarity you have around this, the easier it will be for you to decide where you are going to fit into your industry. Picking this very specific area of your industry is called choosing a "niche," or a specialized segment of your industry.

Choosing a niche is important, as it allows you to develop a very specific brand image, or brand persona, that is going to speak directly to your niche audience. In marketing, we say "If you are not talking to someone specific, you are not talking to anyone." Essentially, this means that there are so many people who are attempting to serve your industry that if you are too broad, you are going to get lost in the noise. People will not know whether you are talking to them personally or not, so they will go find someone else who is clearer with their message and intentions, leaving you struggling to gain any traction in the first place. As you develop an understanding of what your niche is, you give yourself the opportunity to get clear on whom you are talking to and develop an image or a persona that is going to help your audience relate with you. This way, your audience will know to interact with you, and they will begin to see you as the go-to person in your industry to gain the specific tools, services, products, or support that they need based on what you have to offer.

If you are unsure about what specific niches exist in your industry, do not be afraid to run an internet search on niches that are relevant to your industry. Gaining insight from people who are already in the industry is a great chance for you to identify what areas of opportunity exist and how you can fit into those areas.

Some examples of niches include:

- A blog about running shoes
- Eco-friendly reusable products (straws, drink cups, bags, etc.)
- Makeup tutorials for drugstore products
- A designer blog about locally made furniture
- A product review channel for tech gadgets
- Young adult fiction book review blog
- Affordable fashion review blog

As you can see, each of these niche markets has a very clear audience that would be attracted to them based on what it is that they have to offer. The more you can focus on what specifically you will be offering, and to whom, the easier it is for you to create your specific persona. Do not be afraid to get very specific as this is the best opportunity to develop a message that is going to speak directly to your audience.

When you do choose your niche market, there are some things you need to pay attention to. It is important to avoid choosing a niche that is too specific, or one that is not interesting enough for people, as this can lead to you attempting to develop a business in a very limited space. Attempting to serve a niche that does not exist, or where there is not already a healthy audience, can be particularly challenging. Instead, look at existing niches that are thriving and pick a niche that is going to be clear and specific while also being big enough for you to develop into. This ensures that your longevity will remain protected as you develop your business.

Another thing you need to pay attention to is the longevity of your niche, beyond the size of it. Critically consider how long your niche is likely to be around for and whether or not you could seamlessly transition into a new niche, should the need ever arise. This is an important thing to consider, as you are seeking to develop a business and you want to make sure that the business you develop for yourself has the capacity to continue growing over time; otherwise, you may find yourself developing a strong business that burns out in a few years' time when your niche ends up losing traction and falling apart.

Identifying Your Target Audience

As you were identifying your niche, you were already beginning to get a feel for who your target audience might be. For example, if you chose to become a fashion blogger for athletic clothes, you already have a pretty good idea of the fact that your audience members are going to have an interest in sports. However, you also need to consider the fact that your audience is going to need to be more specific than simply having one thing in common if you are going to be able to reach them and grow your business effectively.

When you define your audience, you want to define a specific "character" or individual that is likely to be drawn to your business. Get very clear on who they are, what demographic they are a part of, why they are interested in your business, and what you have to offer them that no one else does. You will have the opportunity to identify your unique selling points in Chapter 2, but for now, focus on getting clear on why your audience is unique to you. The clearer you are on who your audience is, the clearer you can get on how you can serve them, as you will be able to generate a better idea as to what it is that actually interests them. So, by defining who your audience is, you can essentially define what your service is. This can always evolve as you go, but in the meantime, give yourself a starting point so that you can get clear on what you are serving and whom you are serving it to.

Typically, when you develop a customer character, you want to define who your audience is in a way that allows you to know as much as possible about them. Common questions marketers will ask themselves when they are developing their target audience character sheet include:

- Who are they? (Age, gender, location, etc.)
- What is their home life like? (Relationship status, children, animals, home type)
- What is their work life like? (Job role, status, company type)
- What is their income like? (How much do they make? What assets do they have?)
- What are their professional interests?
- How do they spend their free time?
- Where do they spend their time?
- Who are they spending their time with?
- What are their biggest challenges?
- What are their biggest frustrations?
- What are their most common objections?
- What (or who) influences their decisions?
- What outcome or results do they want?
- How do these outcomes or results make them feel?
- What does their purchasing of your product say about them?
- What are their life aspirations and desires?

Knowing the answers to all of these questions helps you know your audience enough that you can develop a message that will very clearly speak to them. It may seem excessive, at first, but as you begin to develop marketing materials later on you will realize that knowing all of this information about your audience is imperative as it helps you develop very specific pieces of content that relate to them.

Chapter 2: Identifying Your Brand Persona

As you are building a personal brand, you need to look at it in two layers. The first layer is the technical stuff that you sorted out in the last chapter, which essentially discussed what the specifics of your business would be. There, you identified what industry you were going to grow into, what niche you would serve, who your audience would be, and what you would be offering to your audience. This part was important for developing the foundation for your business to grow on, as this is how you are going to know what your goals are and whether or not you are achieving them. Now, you need to equip yourself with the tools to actually reach those goals. This is where your brand persona comes in.

Your brand persona is the character or personality of your brand that your audience will interact with. The easiest way to understand this concept is to imagine that your brand's niche, audience, and offerings were the plot of a novel, and your brand persona was the main character. The niche, audience, and offerings would provide the foundation, but without the main character, there would be no way to serve the story to the reader. This is what you are doing with your brand persona: you are developing a main character with whom your target audience can interact, grow to love, and root for. You want your audience to have a "person" in mind (you) that they can relate to and develop a relationship with so that they continue to follow you, pay attention to your offerings, and champion your business.

Developing your brand persona, then, is not too different from developing a character for a novel either. However, here you are not developing an entirely new character, but instead, you are looking for the aspects of your personality that you want to highlight for your brand so that you can have a clear character to present to your target audience. You will be looking for how you can develop your voice, tone, look, personality, story, and more so that it is clear whom you are sharing with your audience.

As you develop your character, keep in mind that you want to develop a character that is both authentic, and that fits with your target niche. You do not want to develop a persona that is too different from who you truly are, as it will feel like you are always acting and it is likely that your audience will see the discrepancies between whom you show up as and whom you claim to be. By honing in on the part of your authentic personality and choosing to amplify that part of your personality, you can ensure that you are connecting with your audience in an authentic way. This way, you can maintain your persona and develop it in a strong and profound manner.

Who You Are and Why You Are Different

The first thing you need to identify when you are developing your brand persona is who you are and why you are different from everyone else in your niche. Consider this as being the foundation for the persona that you will create, as you want to really get into the core of who you are and how you plan to show up for your audience. Here, you want to consider both how you want to show up and how your audience needs you to show up so that you can develop a personality that is relevant to you while also developing one that your audience is likely to respond to. This way, you can develop a personality that feels fun and enjoyable to partake in, and that is well received by the people who are going to be responsible for helping you generate profits in your business!

You want to start the process of developing your persona by getting into the meat of who you are. The best way to do this is to identify some keywords that highlight your personality, your core values, and what your mission is in the world. These three areas of who you are will help give you some insight as to how you show up, what you like to share with the world, and what you can offer to your audience in terms of a personality for them to relate with. The chances are that you have many core values, a few different life goals, and several aspects of your personality that stands out to you. If this is the case, you can focus on identifying your overall personality and all of your values and goals that relate to your industry and the brand that you are building. If you need to narrow it down even further, you can also narrow down which elements of your personality are going to suit your brand the best so that you are really clear on what personality needs to be amplified for your audience.

Once you have gotten into the meat of who you are, you can begin to identify what it is about you that is going to resonate most with your audience. They are most likely looking for something fairly consistent in the industry that you are in, so many of your values, goals, and personality traits are going to overlap with people who are already in your chosen industry. That is totally fine, and to be expected. In fact, if you were *too* different, you may not fit very well into the industry so do not be afraid to be a part of the pack in terms of having a similar persona to those around you.

Now that you have identified the core of who you are and the main elements of what makes you who you are, you can start focusing on where your uniqueness is. At your core, you are likely to be similar to your competition, but there needs to be more about you that helps set you apart from everyone else who is already out there doing the same thing. If you look at those who have climbed to the top of their industries, it is always because they had something different about them that was unique to their brand experience. Those who are not climbing faster are often trying too hard to fit into the industry, so they find themselves being overshadowed by the many others who are showing up with the same manufactured or plain personality that fails to stand out amongst the crowd.

Think about it: if you scroll Instagram's "style" discovery tab, are you more likely to look at the 800 photos that all look the same, or are your eyes going to immediately spot the one or two that are different from the rest? The chances are that your eyes will look for the differences. This is because those who are different or unique stand out to us and catch our eye. They are not like everyone else; they have something that helps set them apart from the crowd, so rather than having our eyes glaze over we actually begin to pay attention to them. For you to really get yourself out there, you need to be that one person who is doing things differently so that people pay attention to you.

Being unique in online space comes in two layers: your appearance and your personality. Since the social media world is highly based on visual aesthetic, you need to have an appearance that is different from everyone else's if you are going to find a way to stand apart from the crowd and develop your uniqueness online. You can develop a unique look by finding one or two aesthetics that you like that are relevant to your brand but not widely used in your industry and use those as your features. For example, Amanda Frances, a self-made millionaire and business coach, highlights cash money and the colors white, gold, and pink as her primary colors. Most people from her audience can identify her by these two things, and these two aesthetics help her stand out from the rest of the business coaches in the online space. Another great example is Kiki Davies from Pursuing Pretty, which is a popular fashion blogging website. Kiki is well known for her bright and lively colors and the outdoor urban-esque photoshoots that she does to highlight her favorite outfits.

By creating a very specific image for your brand, you make it easier for your audience to identify you when they see you online. Those who are new to your page can immediately tell whether or not they enjoy your aesthetic, and those who have followed you for a while will be able to pick you apart from others based on your aesthetic. Furthermore, using consistent imagery like this for your audience can create a great sense of consistency that results in your audience thinking of you when they see things in their day-to-day life that remind them of you. For example, if you love rainbows and you regularly post pictures of rainbows or rainbow colors, your loyal audience members will begin to associate you with rainbows. Therefore, every time they see a rainbow, they will think about you, and they will be inspired to see what you are up to or catch up with you in the online space.

As you choose your two things, make sure that they will relate to your audience in one way or another so your aesthetic matches that which your audience would be looking for. So, if your audience is a professional one, using kittens as part of your aesthetic is probably not going to be helpful in finding whom you are looking for. You need to pick an aesthetic that is going to appeal to your audience while remaining authentic to you and standing apart from the rest of the crowd. If you cannot think of two things quickly, consider checking out your competition and seeing what they are doing to gain some inspiration for how you can set yourself apart. Refrain from allowing yourself to directly copy someone else, as this will cause you to lose your authenticity and will result in you being seen as a copycat. Instead, use their uniqueness as inspiration to find your own thing so that you can begin developing a specific image for yourself that is unique to you.

Identifying Your Voice

In addition to identifying what you want to look like for your audience, you also need to identify how you want to sound, or what you want to be saying to your audience. The tone in which you share with your audience can play a huge role in how you can connect with the people that you are talking to, as can the language. By identifying the right tone and vocabulary to use, you can ensure that you are connecting with your audience in a way that they relate to and receive.

There are two ways that you can identify a voice for your brand: first by identifying what voice you already have, and second by identifying what the most effective voice in your industry is. You will combine these two voices to generate a voice that is authentic to you while still effectively reaching your target audience. By combining these two voices, you can ensure that you still sound like yourself, which makes it easier for you to come across as authentic, while also speaking in a way that generates traction with your audience. At first, it may feel odd or misplaced to attempt to share with your audience in a way that requires you to consider how they are receiving what you are saying, but in time you will find your voice, and it will come easily to you. Below, you are going to discover five easy steps to identify your brand voice so that you can communicate in a way that allows you to have a consistent tone and message for your audience.

Step 1: Read Your Existing Content

The first step in discovering your voice is reading your existing content. Ideally, you want to read content that you have written that is relevant to your industry, but you can also look through your content in general if you have not talked about your industry much, yet. Looking through what you have already written is going to give you the opportunity to get a feel for how you already talk, as well as for how your audience recieves your existing voice.

In addition to reading through your content, read through the content of your competitors and get a feel for how their content comes across. Pay attention to what they sound like, what their personality is, what language they are using, and how their audience is receiving them. Ideally, you want to pay attention to both those who are being well-received and those who are not, as they will both give you excellent information in regards to what is going to work and what won't. Be very attentive to what mannerisms are working and what patterns exist in both types of language, as this is going to help you get clear on what it is that you should do and what you should avoid in order to connect more with your audience.

If you find certain pieces of content that performed well and that you liked, a great idea is to save that piece of content so that you can reference back to it and use it for inspiration later on. This will also help you gain the ability to identify and create your own patterns in your content that allows you to smoothly flow between sharing stories or information and sharing your marketing offers. Typically, most brands use fairly similar formats, though each brand will have its own unique approaches to ensure that they are staying consistent within their content.

Step 2: Describe Your Brand Voice

After you have identified your voice or identified the voice that you like to see most in your competitors, you want to highlight how that voice sounds using three descriptive words. Three descriptive words are necessary as this gives you room to play and create a dynamic voice without going overboard and pulling too many different moving parts into the conversation. The best way to draw out your three words is to go to the content you created or the content you were most inspired by from your competitors and identify three descriptive words that you saw in your content. As you pick your three words, pick them out as though you were describing your brand as a person. For example, use words like passionate, quirky, authentic, professional, genuine, humorous, intelligent, descriptive, or enthusiastic. Keeping your words descriptive and clear allows you to get a feel for what your content should sound like when people are reading it.

Step 3: Create A Voice Chart

Next, you want to create a voice chart. You create a voice chart by taking your three descriptive words and describing how these words are going to show up in your content. For example, if one of your words is passionate, you would write a note about what you are passionate about in particular, and then for how you are going to show your passion in your written content. Perhaps you would show it by using strong verbs, by being champions for your industry, or by cheering people in your industry and your audience on.

Make sure that you create a voice chart for each of the three words that you used to describe your voice with. You can also pick out some industry-specific words that go hand in hand with your chosen descriptive words so that you can get a feel for what language you want to be using in your content. This is a great way to make sure that the language you are using is consistent, relevant, and industry-specific so that your audience can easily receive you.

Step 4: Practice Putting it Into Action

After you have identified what your brand voice sounds like, it is time for you to practice putting it into action. Ideally, you should practice by first writing out some posts for social media in a note on your phone or computer. Get a feel for what it is like to speak in this way, see what you like and do not like, and identify what sounds right for you. Be sure that the content you are creating is valuable and relatable so that your audience can get a strong feel for who you are and what you have to offer them. Read through it and make sure that you have used the words right, that it reads with the proper tone, and that it does not sound too stiff or uncomfortable to read. You want it to come across as friendly and communicative, not planned and overly edited. While it should read as professional and thoughtful, you want to keep it social for *social* media. More often than not, your readers would prefer something that comes across as more raw and authentic than more edited and scripted.

After you have written a few practice pieces, you can begin writing content directly for your audience to read. Post this content on your social media platforms and make sure that you are attentive to how your audience receives it. Try out a few different styles, including different post lengths and goals, and see what your audience receives best. As you begin to accumulate content that they are responding to, keep a track record of your best and worst posts so that you can get a strong understanding of what your audience is looking for. Ideally, you want to create more content like your strongest posts and less content like your weakest posts.

Step 5: Evolve Your Voice

Every person evolves, so your audience is going to expect that you and your brand will evolve too. The best way to evolve your brand is to do so naturally by evolving it alongside yourself. As you grow and your industry grows, naturally incorporate new words and tones into your brand's voice and allow it to adapt and grow alongside your audience. Pay attention to how your audience develops, too, and do not be afraid to incorporate mannerisms and patterns that they use into your language as well.

The best way to ensure that your voice is evolving naturally is to regularly review it to ensure that you are still generating content that works. This may seem overwhelming, but as you get into a routine of checking in on it every three-four months, you will find that it becomes easier and easier. Over time, you will know exactly what to look for, and you will be able to generate content that speaks directly to your audience while evolving alongside them at the same time.

Developing Your Brand Story

Another important part of developing your persona is developing your brand's story. Every brand has a story that contributes to why it came to be a brand in the first place and what inspires it to remain active and growing on a day-to-day basis. This story is what has driven the brand to begin their brand in the first place, and what inspires them to help people in the way that they do. Every single brand uses their story as a way to inform their customers of what they have to offer and how they can offer it in a way that is easy for their customers to receive.

Developing your brand story will be unique, as you are an individual with your own story. You want to make sure that the story you are sharing is authentic to you and your experiences, so you will need to decide to share from a place of personal experience and passion. You also want to make sure that your story is relevant to your audience, so avoid getting into specifics about your past that have nothing to do with your business itself. Instead, get clear on what led you to this point in your business specifically and why you are here serving others. This is the part of your story that your audience wants to hear about, and the part of your story that is going to be relatable to them and their experiences.

The best way to develop the story that you will be sharing is, first, to get clear on how your story benefits your audience. Pay attention to what aspects of your experiences and history are relatable to your audience and allow those parts to come together as your story. Then, pay attention to how your story reads. Your story and your tone need to read together effectively, so you want to make sure that you are being intentional in bringing your tone into your story. Read through your story a few times and see how it relates to your audience, how it reads, and whether or not it uses the right language to reach your audience effectively.

Your story is going to be used in several ways, so once you have written your main story and edited through it to ensure that it reads effectively to your audience, you are going to want to keep that. You may choose to place it on your website for your audience to read, or you may wish to keep it to yourself and use it as inspiration for your marketing strategies as you go forward. Either way, having this story available is going to ensure that the general message of your brand always stays on target and that you are always consistent with your story and the information that you are sharing with your audience.

When it comes to marketing from your story, you will want to create pieces of marketing material that are relevant to the story that you are sharing. Make sure that it relates to your story, that it is a part of your story, or that it contributes to people understanding your story and becoming a part of your solution or resolve. This is the best way to ensure that all of your materials stay on-brand and relevant to your audience.

Dancing Between Your Persona and Your Audience

The final part of developing a persona is learning how to maintain your persona while also evolving to meet the needs of your audience. When it comes to developing a personal brand, it can be easy to get lost in trying to meet the demands of your audience and losing the footing that you have in being yourself. Particularly in a brand that is developed on yourself, it can sometimes be challenging to remember that you are not required to shift or change who you are to meet the needs of your audience. You are allowed to, and in fact, you are required to, continue being yourself in order to really allow your brand to flourish. Brands who try too hard to meet the needs of their audience almost always end up losing themselves and find themselves struggling to really stand out and meet their audience's needs. Your audience needs you to stay focused on who you are and to continue showing up in a powerful way so that you can remain the influential persona that they have come to enjoy. For that reason, you need to learn how to walk the line of staying strong and authentic while also evolving and shifting with and for your audience. This comes with a bit of practice.

To continue showing up as your authentic self, it is important always to reflect on every post that you are about to share and determine whether or not it truly sounds like you. If it does not sound like it is something that you would genuinely share, then it is likely a good idea to avoid sharing that content. If you share content that does not sound like something you would write, you will find yourself sharing content that does not resonate well with your audience. And if on the off chance it does, you may begin to feel as though you are required to step away from your authentic voice to serve your audience's needs. Both of these scenarios are not ideal.

Instead, seek to share content that sounds and feels right for what you would be sharing, and that continues to have your personality and voice in it. Do not be afraid to keep your content raw and real, and do not feel like you have to overedit anything or put too much pressure into being someone that your audience needs you to be. Remember: they do need you to be a certain person, but they need you to be more of a leader and less of a follower. That means that you need to know how to be your authentic self and anticipate their needs through your authenticity, not speak exactly as they do and become exactly who they are.

That being said, you do want to stay relevant with your audience by continuing to show up for them in a way that they can receive. This means that you need to be able to identify trends in your industry and follow those trends so that you can stay relevant. If a shift in language occurs, or some new topic or item comes into style, you need to be staying on top of these things and incorporating them into your authentic image. Find a way to bring them in through your own unique strategy and voice so that your audience sees that you are staying relevant while also staying authentic to who you are.

In addition to anticipating and incorporating shifts in language and trending topics or items, make sure that you are also evolving as a person. People typically like to follow personal brands that are continuing to evolve as individuals, as they enjoy watching a person grow through life and achieve their goals. They want to relate to you as though you are their friend, so your audience wants to see you setting goals and winning. Do not be afraid to talk about your aspirations and share your wins with your audience, as this allows you to share a unique experience with them in which they get to celebrate you for your wins. It also shows them what is possible and invites them to share their wins with you so that you can celebrate them as well. This back-and-forth connection between you and your audience is a powerful opportunity for you to make sure that you are building those relationships with your audience and evolving them over time. The more you develop these connections and grow, the more powerful you will become and the more your brand will grow.

Chapter 3: Facebook Marketing

Facebook is the largest social media platform in 2019, which makes it a powerful tool for anyone who is seeking to develop their brand online. That being said, you need to know how to use Facebook in 2019 to really leverage this platform and start getting your name out there. Facebook has become its own online community with many different hangout spots for people to spend time connecting with friends, family, and even strangers who are interested in similar things. From Facebook profiles and business pages to groups, there are many different ways that you can develop a presence on Facebook and start generating traction on this mega platform.

Ideally, if you want to start developing your presence on Facebook, you should be prepared to spend at least 30-45 minutes per day on this platform learning about how it works and engaging with your audience. This gives you plenty of time to understand how the platform works, to put out new content, and to engage with the people who are engaging with your content. That way you not only build up a presence but you also begin to build up social connections, which is something that people on Facebook value deeply. In this chapter, we are going to explore how you can leverage Facebook's vast community to help you generate an online presence for your brand.

Benefits of Facebook for Personal Brands

Facebook has a wide range of benefits that it offers to brands who choose to use this platform to begin connecting with their audience. The biggest benefit of using Facebook is that this platform has many different demographics existing on it, making it an excellent location to tap into just about any target audience. You can leverage your Facebook profile for many different things, from developing an influencer account to actually growing a small business and selling products or services to your audience. How you choose to develop your Facebook account is largely up to you.

Aside from the broad range of people who are actively using Facebook every single day, there are many other benefits to Facebook as well. For example, Facebook has optimized its platform for the business to customer connection, making it an excellent platform for anyone who is trying to connect with customers. From creating business pages that can be developed with plenty of great content to connect with your audience, to developing a group which offers a private community for you and your followers to hang out in, there are several ways that you can connect with your audience. Beyond traditional posting, Facebook also offers 24-hour story feeds and private messages so that you can offer even more exclusive connection opportunities for your audience.

When you are developing your brand, having at least a small presence on Facebook is ideal, as many people who are interested in researching a brand or business will search them on Facebook, or Instagram. Ensuring that you have an existing presence on Facebook helps people see that you are a legitimate business and that you can be connected with through social platforms, which is an ideal situation for most modern people. Another reason why having the ability to connect with you online is beneficial to your audience is that your audience has the opportunity to see your business' reviews on Facebook. Early on this may mean nothing, but as you begin to develop more clients and those clients review you online, Facebook provides a great place for your audience to see those reviews and determine whether or not they want to work with you.

Finally, Facebook is a social sharing site which values authentic content, which means that getting on Facebook gives you the opportunity to express yourself in a unique and personalized manner. When people follow you, they can comment on and react to your content which gives them a chance to feel as though they are developing a personal relationship with you. This helps your audience feel far more connected with you, which results in them experiencing a greater sense of loyalty to you and your brand.

Using A Public Profile

Using a public profile is a great way to begin developing a connection with your audience if you are developing a personal brand, as this gives a very personal feel. Public profiles are essentially personal profiles that have all of their security settings set to public so that anyone can see and follow you on Facebook. In general, these types of profiles allow people to feel far more connected with you because they feel as though they are genuinely becoming your friends and not just your followers. As a result, they are more likely to pay attention to what you are sharing, engage with you, and develop a relationship with you in the online space.

If you use a public profile, it is important that you ensure that every piece of content being shared on that profile is well branded. You do not want to be sharing content that is too personal, or that is irrelevant to your brand, as this can result in you having a platform that is confusing and that causes your followers to feel unclear about who you are and what you have to offer online. Instead, make sure that the aesthetic of your profile and the overall messages all follow the same theme of your brand, so that people get a feel for who you are and remain consistent in what that feeling is. You can definitely shine your authenticity through and share small pieces of your more personal life with your audience to give them that intimate connection that the social media world likes, but ensure that you continue to remain private about who you are. You do not want to put every single aspect of your life on social media, only to find it being held against you or holding you back in the long run.

Furthermore, make sure that your personal profile contains a healthy mixture of shared content and personally created content. Sharing other people's content is a great opportunity to build out your profile and share more of who you are, but if you are not generating enough personally curated content, you are missing an opportunity. In generating your own content, you give people the opportunity to get a strong feel for who you are and what you share so that they can decide whether or not they want to follow you.

Lastly, make sure that your personal profile *feels* personal. Do not just use your profile's wall to market to your audience in every single post. Generate buzz, share interesting content, engage with your audience, and develop a personality online that they can relate to. The more you work toward building yourself up as a genuine person online, the more people are going to personally relate to you and experience interest in and loyalty toward your brand. That way, people are more likely to actually make a purchase when they begin to see you posting about your latest offers.

Using A Business Page

Facebook business pages work almost like personal profiles, except that you can gear them more toward your business. Business pages can be named after your brand or your small business, have an "About" section that you can fill out to provide information to your audience and have the opportunity to have many other functional tabs added to the page. For example, you can add a shopping tab, a services tab, a tab that provides access to video content, or even a tab that allows people to leave reviews on your business. Ideally, you should utilize any tabs that are relevant to your brand to ensure that you can fill out your business page with plenty of information about who you are and what your brand is all about. This way, people can get as much information as they need to decide whether or not your brand is the one that they want to do business with.

Another benefit to having a business page is that you can keep it entirely business-oriented. Instead of needing to make it more personal and friendly as you would on a personal profile, you can make your business page more professional. You can use a business-related or professional profile picture, header image, and username for your profile so that everything has a more professional feel to it. More of your posts can be geared toward marketing, you can offer links to various products and services that you have available, and you can keep people up-to-date in regards to the goings-on of your business.

When you develop your business page, it is a good idea to keep the type of content that you share varied. Ideally, every piece of content should have some form of a photograph or graphic attached to it to ensure that your profile is visually interesting. If you can create video content, such as a live video or a recorded video, this is a great tool as well as the Facebook demographic tends to love consuming video content. You can share video content about everything from your latest products and services to updates that are relevant to your followers. The more video-related content you share, the more your audience can connect with you on a face-to-face level and feel a sense of personal connection with you.

Running Advertisements

After you have developed your business page and filled out all of your information and tabs, you can also use your business page to begin running advertisements on Facebook. Advertisements are a powerful tool that can help you access more of your target audience faster, making it easier for you to begin to develop your presence on Facebook. Advertising can also be used to market your products and services and gain better traction from your sales, which makes it an excellent tool to use on Facebook. Another great benefit to Facebook's advertising platform is that it runs Instagram's advertising platform as well since Facebook owns Instagram. As a result, you can use one platform to run ads on two platforms, making it an excellent time saver, and keeping everything organized.

When it comes to Facebook advertising, the stats are promising which makes this an excellent platform for you to advertise on. 93% of marketers are using Facebook advertising on a regular basis because it enables them to access such a large segment of their target audience for a relatively low cost. When you learn how to get your ROI strong, which is not too hard to do, you can discover how to develop advertisements that generate massive conversions in a fairly minimal amount of time.

Creating Facebook advertisements that work does take some practice, but once you understand it, you can develop a strong ad set that converts quickly. One of the biggest things that you can do for your platform to start generating conversions is to use images, as images are known for helping generate traction. Ads that are promoted without images rarely perform well, so 75-90% of Facebook ads are accompanied by an image or graphic of some sort. You also need to make sure that the copy that you write for your advertisement can gain someone's attention within the first three seconds, as people will rapidly lose interest and stop paying attention if you don't.

When it comes to generating the back end of the ad, there are two simple techniques that you can use to identify your target audience and target your audience effectively. First, you want to identify your target audience based on who is already following your page and who interacts with you on a consistent basis. If you are not getting consistent traction yet, refrain from paid advertising until your organic advertising stats are higher so that you know exactly whom you need to target with your campaigns. This way, you do not waste any money trying to guess who your demographic is. In addition to getting an idea for who your demographic is through who is engaging with your content, you can also pay attention to who else they are interacting with so that you can get a clear idea of what they are interested in. By targeting your demographic based on their demographic category as well as what their other interests are, you can increase your likelihood of connecting with hot leads in your target audience.

On Facebook's advertising platform, getting your advertisements created is incredibly simple. You start by logging into your advertisement account or tapping the "Promote" button at the top of your business page, and you begin following the step-by-step instructions on the screen to develop your ad. You will be walked through the process of choosing your objective, naming your campaign, developing the design for your campaign, and highlighting whom you want your campaign to be seen by the most. Once you have done that, all you have to do is choose your budget, how long you want your campaign to run, and then you simply promote your campaign.

Facebook Groups

Facebook groups are an excellent place to hang out with your audience and develop personal connections with them online. This is also an excellent opportunity for your community to connect and collaborate, which can develop an even stronger loyalty toward you as your community realizes that you are the common denominator that has brought them all together. As a result, your community gains value not only from you but from each other as well, which draws even greater intensity into your brand.

If you are using a Facebook group for your business, it is a good idea to choose a group that clearly works alongside what you promote with your business, and that offers value. For example, if you are a make-up artist, running a group that has exclusive tutorials and promotions is a great opportunity to build a community and offer value into that community so that your followers have an incentive to join and be an active part of it.

In your Facebook group, it is a good idea to check in on a consistent basis, offer valuable content, and comment on other people's posts within your group. The more time you spend engaging and interacting with your audience, the more you will be able to have your audience connect with you and generate a personal relationship with you through Facebook. This is perhaps the biggest benefit to your audience, too, in that being a part of your Facebook group feels like an exclusive "in" where they get to hang out with you and be a part of your "circle" online. This is even more exclusive than being your Facebook friend, which can make being a part of your world more fun and exciting for anyone who is a part of it.

Connecting with Fellow Influencers

On Facebook, one of the best things that you can do for yourself is to develop relationships with influencers who are a part of the same industry as you are. Influencers who are in your industry, particularly those who are already more established, are great friends to have as they can support you in your growth. The modern online business community fosters community over competition, so for that reason becoming a part of the community can be a powerful business move for you. Identify who the key players in your industry are, join their groups, follow them or friend them, and begin interacting with their content regularly. This will not only give you the opportunity to continue creating more relationships online, but it will also support you in accessing inspiration for how you can develop and grow in your business.

As you do befriend those from your own industry online, make sure that all of your connections are genuine and heartfelt. Do not attempt to generate connections just so that you can gain intel and start copying your fellow industry influencers, as this can result in you looking fake and losing credibility. Furthermore, if an influencer spots that you are doing this, the word may get out, and your reputation may be tarnished by your less than genuine intentions. Instead, be genuine in your intentions by truly creating and establishing meaningful relationships within your industry and growing alongside the people who are on a similar path as you are.

Beyond supporting you with your business itself, being connected with people who are doing the same things as you are is a great way to really create a sense of comradery in your life. Being an entrepreneur can be lonely at times, so having people who can relate to you is excellent for you to feel as though you are supported and understood. This way, anytime you are going through a hardship, or you want to bring even more community into your business and life, you know whom you can turn to and rely on. Make sure that you return the favor to the influencers that you care to remain friends with so that your relationships are nourished and plentiful, rather than one-sided and unfair.

Growth Hack: Interacting on Facebook

Facebook is one platform where social interaction is extremely important. People who "post and dash" or who leave a post or a link somewhere and then never do anything else are often frowned upon and forgotten about on Facebook. Facebook's algorithm and its users prefer individuals who post content, comment back to those who are sharing on the content, and who engage with other peoples' content. For that reason, genuine social connection and time spent communicating with others is a powerful opportunity for you to connect with people who are relevant to your industry and grow on Facebook.

The more you share conversations with people on Facebook, the more that your followers are going to see that you are genuine and interesting. As a result, they will discover that you are fun to engage with and they will be more likely to continue engaging with you and sharing you with their circle who may also be interested in your content. The more you do this, the more you will grow organically, and the more loyal your following will become. Even larger influencers continue to take the time to engage with their audience in a genuine and heartfelt way, so do not allow yourself ever to reach the point where you feel like a genuine connection is beyond you. Instead, see how valuable these relationships are in your life and always put the work into growing them so that you can continue valuing and nurturing your audience in a powerful and personal manner.

Chapter 4: Instagram Marketing

Instagram is currently one of the most popular platforms for influencers to partake in when they are developing an image in the online space. Instagram is largely based on aesthetic and appearance, and the power of using strong captions to capture people's attention and draw them into your personal brand. When you combine the design element and the written element of Instagram effectively, Instagram can be leveraged as a powerful tool to support you in developing a platform for your brand so that you can connect with your audience in a bigger way.

One of the biggest reasons why Instagram is so valuable to influencers is because the reality of influencers is something that is largely experienced amongst the younger crowd. Typically, influencers are in their 20s and 30s and are being followed by people who are roughly the same age as they are. Older generations are not using influencers so often, nor do they fully comprehend the value that an influencer can bring to both companies and their followers. Since Instagram largely caters to those who are in their 20s and 30s as well, it makes sense that this platform is powerful for those who are amongst this demographic. Even if you are not seeking to be an influencer alone, but instead you want to be a service provider or product creator with influential power, getting into Instagram's atmosphere is a great opportunity to spread your wings in front of your target audience.

Benefits of Using Instagram

As social media develops, people are finding that they are more drawn to visual content than ever before. Photographs are powerful, as are videos. The more you step into using photographs and videos to support you in providing aesthetic content for your audience, the more you are going to develop a personal connection with your audience. Instagram allows people to take advantage of visual advertising by hosting pages that are entirely based on photographs, with captions added beneath them. They also offer 24-hour stories, IGTV, and live video streams. The more you engage in these different forms of visual sharing, the more your page will grow, and people will be able to follow you.

Another great benefit to Instagram is that it is easier for people to find you based on what you share and how you tag your photographs. On apps like Facebook, people need to find your account through their friends or through a mutual group that you are involved in; otherwise, they have no way of finding you. On Instagram, people can search for hashtags, and as long as your picture has been tagged with it, they can find you. This is how they can like your content and, if they like it a lot, begin following you. This makes it far easier for people to be funneled to your page through your photographs, making it a more effective platform to grow on.

Lastly, Instagram can be interconnected with Facebook, so if you want to host both a Facebook and Instagram page to maximize your viewership, you can do so through connecting the two accounts. This way, anything you share on Instagram can be shared on Facebook, and you can manage your ad accounts through Facebook for Instagram too. This makes it easy for you to manage two accounts effortlessly so that you can develop your online platform and begin making a larger impact without having it take up quite so much time.

Developing Your Profile

To have a strong presence on Instagram, you need to learn how to develop an effective profile that is going to help you get views and increase your followers. The key with developing a profile on Instagram is keeping it attractive without making your profile look like every other profile that is on the platform right now. Recently, a trend for alternating between quotes and images rose, and within a few months, everyone was using this aesthetic, which resulted in people's accounts all looking the same. This is where having your unique edge is powerful: it allows you to stop trying to create an aesthetic that fits in and start creating one that actually looks like your brand.

It is important that as you seek to stand out on Instagram, you also continue to remain true to your brand. We will talk more about keeping your profile authentic below, but for now, you should know that it is important for you to develop an aesthetic that is attractive and authentic. You are going to do this by developing a branded profile through the steps below.

First, brand the basics of your account. Begin by creating a branded username and a branded profile picture. Your username should be either your business name or your name, which will keep it simple and easy to find. If your name is already in use, you can consider adding something small to it to make yourself easier to locate, though if you do this, you are going to want to be consistent by using the same username across all platforms so that you are easy to locate everywhere. Your profile image should be of you, or your logo if you run a small business. Personal brands should also always use a personal photograph, as this keeps them easy to identify and keeps the account looking personable and friendly. Make sure that the photograph you use is relevant to your profile so that it makes sense; otherwise, people may not know to follow you, or they may think that your brand is too confusing to understand. For example, if you market yourself as a make-up artist, but you are taking shots in your profile picture, people are not going to have any clue as to what it is that you are trying to market. Instead, you would want to have a relevant picture, such as one of you applying your makeup or wearing a bold makeup look. Using relevant images helps keep your page branded so that people know what to expect with you.

The second step is designing your bio and your website link. Your bio should be a simple description of who you are and what you have to offer so that your audience knows what they are getting when they come to your page. Most professional individuals' bio will have their professional title, mission, and potentially something that they are interested in or something that sets them apart. For example, if you are a vegan chef with a passion for animal rights, you might share a bio that says "Plant-Powered Vegan Chef, Saving One Chicken Little at A Time." Having a bio that shows off what your mission is, what you are interested in, and what it is that you do give your audience an idea of who you are in just moments of landing on your page.

If you are unsure about how you should write your bio or what you should include in yours, take a look at your fellow influencers' pages and see how they have written their bios so that you can get a feel for what you like. As you do, start piecing together a bio that sounds more authentic to your brand. You can use elements of other bios that you liked as a way to develop the format for your bio—then you can simply begin to fill in your personal information. Once you have come across something you like, measure it against your brand's voice and persona to ensure that you have created a bio that sounds authentic. Then, simply use that!

For your link, you can do virtually anything that you desire. If you want, you can link your followers to your website where you offer your products or services, or you can link them to a different online profile that you use more frequently. For example, if you are typically on YouTube sharing videos, linking to your YouTube from your Instagram account is a great way to drive more traffic to your preferred platform. Another great usage for the link in your bio is if you find that you have several links that you want to share, such as links to your other social media platforms, your website, or latest offerings, you can always use a landing page app like LinkTree. LinkTree is free and enables you to link multiple links to one landing page so that you can send your followers to a variety of different places depending on what they are looking for. This is excellent for anyone who has multiple offers and wants to offer them all through Instagram.

Lastly, you are going to need to design your newsfeed itself. Your newsfeed is where you get to share pictures with your audience, and the pictures you say immediately tell a story about your brand. For that reason, you want to share pictures that are going to be relevant to your brand so that people see your page and immediately get a feel for who you are. The best way to do this is to refer back to the aesthetic you identified when you were developing your brand persona and begin generating an aesthetic around this appearance for your profile. Sometimes it can take some time to develop an aesthetic that serves your brand, so do not be afraid to develop your aesthetic over time so that you can get a feel for what you like and what you do not like.

If you are unsure about where to start when it comes to developing your aesthetic, do not be afraid to look to your competitors and begin developing an aesthetic that matches what your competitors are using. You do not want to recreate the same aesthetic, but getting a feel for how others are wielding their unique edge can be beneficial in helping you get a sense for how you can use your own. Over time, you will find your stride, and it will become easier for you to determine what your audience likes and how you can develop content that actually interests them so that they continue paying attention to your page. After you have developed your aesthetic, all you need to do is maintain your page!

Keeping Your Profile Authentic

On Instagram, one of your most powerful tools is your authenticity. Because Instagram is so popular for influencers, many wannabes have popped up and started developing generic pages that look just like the successful influencer's pages as an attempt to become popular themselves. When your page is too stiff or has been manufactured too specifically, you can drive your audience away as it begins to feel like your page is not authentic. On Instagram, there is a thing called "bots", which is essentially programs that are designed to develop pages and run those pages so that businesses can make money without actually doing anything on the platform. Not only are bots typically weeded out by Instagram itself, but they also develop very generic and uninteresting profiles that are not effective in helping people grow their pages. In the end, these pages look like they are too similar to all of the other Instagram pages out there, which results in them struggling to develop any traction. If you want to grow, you need to keep your unique appearance available for your audience to follow; otherwise, it will not work.

The best way to create an authentic and attractive feed is to think about your message, your story, and your offerings and create images and captions that fit directly into this feel. Then, you want to choose an aesthetic that fits this message as well. As you choose your images, make sure that they follow the general aesthetic that you are creating and that they go together with the images around them. So, they should match the image that will come immediately after them and the one that will fall below them. The more coherent your feed is, the more attractive it will be, so pay attention to keeping similar themes in terms of what is in your image, what colors you are using, and how they are sharing your message with the people around you.

Hashtagging and Geotagging

On Instagram, the way to have your images seen is to have hashtags and geotags activated on your images so that your images can be located. If you are not already aware of how things work on Instagram, hashtags are tags that you use to categorize your photographs in the app's algorithm, and geotags are how you categorize yourself based off of location. If you want to grow your platform and get discovered by people who are going to become your followers and, eventually, your clients, you need to be making effective use of hashtags and geotags to get yourself discovered.

Hashtags are the primary discovery tool on Instagram, so you will want to use hashtags as your main method for getting discovered by new followers. One of the best ways to start finding hashtags for Instagram is to begin using keywords in your hashtags. That being said, you do want to be rather specific in the keywords that you are using, as using larger or broader keywords can result in you being quickly buried by the thousands of other people who are using these keywords, also. To give you a greater understanding, each time a hashtag is used the recent list is updated with that new picture. So, if hundreds or thousands of people are using a hashtag per hour, your image can get buried quickly, resulting in you not being discovered as easily. Likewise, if you are using a hashtag that is fairly irrelevant or that no one is searching for, you need to understand that said hashtag may not work in helping you discover anyone new since no one will actively be looking for that hashtag.

Finding the right hashtags to use can be made easier by doing an Instagram search, or by downloading a tool like PLANN or Iconosquare. If you want to search for new hashtags directly on Instagram, going to the discover page and keying in your keyword is a great way for you to discover what else people are searching for when they search for your keyword. You can discover more by either looking in the "related" section and discovering new hashtags or by looking at the hashtags that other people are using. If you are going to look at other people's posts for inspiration, you should focus on finding posts that look similar to the ones that you are sharing so that you can ensure that the hashtags you begin using are going to be populated with content like what you are sharing. If you attempt to use hashtags where your content is irrelevant, you are going to find that you do not gain much traction as you are being seen as irrelevant and disinteresting on these categories. Instead, people will likely think that you are out of place and will begin to ignore you and everything that you share.

In addition to choosing the right hashtags that are going to gain you traction, you also want to use geotags as much as possible to help you gain traction as well. When you have geotags turned on for your photographs, it shows people who are in your area your images, which can help you gain more local traffic. You can also use geotag locations for popular hangouts such as restaurants, tourist spots, or other attractions, as these will help you gain more traction by showing your audience where you are. Furthermore, if you geotag locations, you have a higher chance of being regrammed (or having your image shared) by a popular account that may already have a significant number of followers. If this happens, you will find that you can get even more traction on your posts as people begin seeing your photographs being shared by other popular accounts, making it easier for them to find you. Even if they do not share your picture, tagging people, locations, or other relevant accounts in your images can be a great opportunity to increase your number of followers by making it easier for people to find you.

On Instagram, you can use up to one geotag and up to 30 hashtags, as well as up to 30 tags in an image. You should aim to use all of your geotags and hashtags as often as possible to ensure that you are getting found, so long as the hashtags that you are using are relevant. Refrain from tagging too many other accounts too frequently in your posts, as this can often look spammy. However, if you do have someone or something relevant that you can tag in your post, you can always tag them to increase your traction and grow your account even faster.

Growth Hack: Step-by-Step Guide for Instagram Growth

There are many strategies that you can tap into to help you grow on Instagram. Ideally, you want to get your growth strategy sorted out in a way that makes it simple and consistent so that you can continue growing on a regular basis. The more streamlined your growth strategy is, the simpler it will be for you to develop your account and grow faster. Below is an excellent growth strategy that you can put into place to help you begin growing your account rapidly, and you can adjust it as you see fit to help your unique channel grow even faster. To access all of the tools and information being provided in this strategy, you will want to turn on the business features on your Instagram account. You can do this by going into your settings, tapping "Account" and then tapping "Switch to Business Account". Once you have turned this feature on, you can begin tracking information, such as your analytics, which will be important for helping you develop your account even further.

Step 1: Create Hashtag Pods

Hashtag pods are essentially procreated groups of hashtags that you can use to help you have your hashtags readily available for when it comes time to post any new content on your page. Having hashtags already researched and saved is a great opportunity to streamline your posting process by giving you easy access to a set of hashtags that you can use with all of your new posts. Creating hashtag pods does not have to be challenging, either, as you can create them by following the research methods above and then categorizing them based on what types of photographs you typically share online. If you are the type to share the same type of content regularly, or if you find that your hashtag needs will switch up with each post, you can always compile a list of your most commonly used hashtags and keep that list handy. That way, each time you post, you simply need to select the hashtags that are most relevant to your new post and use those.

Step 2: Find Your Peak Posting Times

One big benefit of having your Instagram business analytics turned on is that you can pay attention to when your peak posting times are on Instagram. Peak posting times essentially mean the times that your pictures are most likely to be engaged with on Instagram. Each brand has its own unique peak posting times, so you will want to discover what yours are and then use these peak times as your opportunity to get traction on your Instagram. The best way to begin this process is to spend a few weeks sharing pictures at any time throughout the day, without paying much attention to this analytic at first. Try to post at varying points throughout each day so that you are more likely to get a more well-rounded idea of what your peak times are. Then, after a few weeks, note down these peak times and begin intentionally posting around them. The more you intentionally post around your peak times, the better your traction is going to be, as Instagram favors posts that gain a lot of traction quickly after being posted.

Step 3: Monitor Your Content Performance

You should always pay attention to how your content is performing when you post new content, as this is how you can ensure that you are being seen by the maximum number of people with each new post. When you post, pay attention to how much traction you get within 20 minutes, 12 hours, 24 hours, and 48 hours. Take note of any posts that continue to gain traction for longer than 48 hours, as these posts are typically the ones that are most liked by your audience. By getting a feel for what your audience likes the most, you can ensure that everything you are posting is being effectively received by your audience. Doing this enables you to ensure that every single thing you post is relevant, interesting, and going to maximize the amount of traction that you gain from your audience.

Step 4: Engage Frequently

Instagram is a social media account, which means that the amount of interaction you get often equals to the amount that you give. This does not mean that you have to be on Instagram for hours every day paying attention to the people you are following and searching for new people, but it does mean that you should be spending time every single day interacting with your existing followers and potential new followers. Getting active on your account and liking and commenting on people's content is a great opportunity to get found by more people, which enables your account to grow faster. Not only does it put your name in their notifications feed, but it puts your name out there in front of their audience, while also driving your account up in the Instagram algorithm. Essentially, the more you post and engage, the more Instagram sees you as being relevant and begins sharing your posts with more people.

Step 5: Adjust Your Approach as Needed

Since your Instagram account is being used for business purposes, it is a good idea that you approach it like a business and begin learning how you can develop your growth strategies with it. You can do this by regularly revisiting your existing approach to Instagram to ensure that it is still working out in your favor. The more you pay attention to your growth and continue to understand what it is that your audience is looking for, the more you are going to have to offer your audience, making it even easier for you to continue growing. As long as you continue approaching your profile with the intention of serving your audience, your growth is going to be sustainable and continual. If you are unsure about how you can approach your growth strategy to ensure that you are using the most effective approach at all times, you can easily begin by setting a recurring date for when you want to review your profile. You may wish to review your profile weekly, bi-weekly, monthly, or even quarterly to see how your overall growth is doing and to ensure that you are using the most effective methods possible. If you are choosing to set your date to something more frequent, such as weekly, make sure that any changes you instill are gradual to ensure that you are not shifting things faster than your audience can reasonably respond to. Ideally, you should leave a new method in place for at least a few weeks to ensure that you are gaining reasonable analytics that are truly reflective of whether or not your audience enjoys the content that you are putting out.

Chapter 5: Twitter Marketing

Twitter is another major social media platform that is well known for being a great place to grow your presence online. Most major influencers have an established presence on Twitter, as Twitter allows them to engage in genuine back-and-forth conversations with their audience in a massive way. This is also a great platform for anyone who is targeting a more mature audience, as most of Twitter's audience is comprised of people who are over the age of 30, which means that you can easily access an older demographic here. Getting on Twitter allows you to begin engaging with your audience in an entirely new way, as Twitter still largely consists of status updates and conversations, more so than anything else. This can be an excellent platform for generating relationships with your audience so that you can continue to develop your shared relationships.

Many people tend to either love or hate Twitter, so if you have yet to develop a positive experience with the platform, give yourself the time to learn how to use it and trust that once you figure it out, it does become much more enjoyable. Because of the dynamic, some people find it to be a challenge to get discovered or heard on Twitter, which is reasonable when you consider that this particular platform operates so differently from any other platform online. Using the strategies that you learn about in this chapter, you are going to discover how you can use Twitter in an effective way that allows you to create a more powerful impact with your followers.

Benefits of Using Twitter

Twitter is an incredibly powerful platform for anyone who is seeking to connect more with their audience. This platform has evolved to be one of the best business to customer platforms as it enables businesses to develop meaningful relationships with their audience through not only posting but also engaging in actual conversations with their followers. Beyond that, Twitter has been known to be used as a platform to manage customer service inquiries and complaints about clients who are not particularly pleased with the service that they have received with any particular company. As a result, Twitter has become known as a great platform for anyone who is looking to start working together with their audience to develop a greater impact on their business and influence.

Beyond offering the opportunity to develop greater relationships with your audience, Twitter is also known for being one of the most effective platforms for those who are interested in creating more traffic for their websites. Statistics have shown that 80% of all people who land on someone's Twitter profile will go on to click the link that they have provided in their bio. This means that Twitter is an incredible way to funnel people from your profile to your website, or anywhere else where they may be able to learn more about your business and then buy a product or service from you.

Developing Your Twitter Profile

Since Twitter can be such a strong element of any online sales funnel, developing your Twitter profile effectively is important. You need to make sure that all of the elements of your profile are optimized so that anyone who lands on your profile can see that you are, in fact, interesting for them. You can optimize your Twitter profile by focusing on five simple aspects of your page, which you will want to optimize when you first launch your account and then maintain as you continue to develop your page.

When you first launch your page, you want to look at the branding perspective to ensure that your profile is effectively branded. You will want to adjust your username to reflect your brand, update your profile picture to either your face or your logo, and add your website into the bio section so that your audience can go to your website should they desire to. These three basic areas will ensure that your page has the basic set up required to manage a great Twitter page online.

The next thing you want to do after launching your profile is to update your cover image. You want to keep your cover image updated by regularly adding a new one, as your cover image is a great tool to use when it comes to marketing. Many Twitter users will feature their latest offering or sale in their cover image, which allows anyone who lands on their profile to instantly see what they have to offer and begin generating interest in that offer. Since most offerings are seasonal or time sensitive, paying attention to your picture and updating it regularly is important to avoid having an out-of-date image on your feed. If your image is out of date, you might find that you have people looking away from your page because it seems as though you are not attentive or maintaining your account very well. Alternatively, you may have people requesting that you honor outdated sales pricing or offers because you have advertised for it on your Twitter page.

If you do choose to use time-sensitive cover images that you will update regularly, it is a good idea to make a note of the date that they need to be switched by in your calendar. This way, you can be reminded that it is time to create a new picture and update your profile, to avoid having your profile going out of season. If you find that you have a hard time keeping up with this, you may benefit from having a more generic picture that you can use so that you are not required to update your picture quite as often. Even so, you may want to update your cover image from time to time so that your page looks fresh and new when people land on it.

When you do design your cover image, make sure that you have designed it in a way so that all of the information can be seen on your profile. A common mistake people make on their profiles is uploading images that have important information on the cover image that is covered by the person's profile image. As a result, you cannot see what it is that you are supposed to do, or when the event runs from, or other important information that you would need access to in order to act on their marketing information. If you are not familiar with how to design a cover image, you can always use Canva or Photoshop as a platform to customize your profile image. Once you find a template that works, you can save that template and customize it anytime you are uploading a new image to your Twitter so that you can be sure that your image will always be professional and proportionate.

Your bio is an important tool that you should be using to let your audience know who you are, what you have to offer, and what they can expect from you. On Twitter, you have 160 characters to write your bio, so while you cannot include a lot of information here, you can summarize your profile fairly well. Your bio can be customized in almost any way that feels right for your unique brand, as long as the information in it is clear and supports your audience in being able to understand what it is that you have to offer.

Some great examples of bios include ones like:

- "Adventure into brand visibility and build your audience so that you can build your business."
- "Marketer with love for cappuccino art and awesome hair."
- "White collar income with a redneck soul."
- "#1 Content Marketing Influencer, Social Media Marketing Strategist & Speaker, Forbes Top 10 Social Media Influencer, #1 Global Business Blog."

Having a clear and interesting bio gives your audience a clear understanding of who you are and why they should follow you. It can also encourage them to find their way to your website so that they can book a service or purchase a product, depending on what you have to offer.

Twitter offers you the opportunity to pin Tweets, which can be a valuable tool if you are interested in helping your audience find certain pieces of information easier. For example, if you are running a sale, have a favorite quote, or want to offer a favorite tip, you can use the pinned Tweet as an opportunity to show that information at the top of your profile. Since pinned Tweets tend to get more engagement than any other Tweet, you want to make sure that the pinned Tweet you choose is optimized for your audience. You can do this by including a high-quality image that is 1024 x 512 pixels, to avoid having any part of the image cut off. If you are directing people to your website, make sure that you also include a clickable link or a clear call to action to have people go to the link in your bio, and then have that link be the correct one based on what you are asking your followers to do.

Lastly, if you are going to use hashtags on your Tweets, make sure that you are using the best ones. Twitter's more recent updates mean that you no longer have to use hashtags as it will sort your posts out based on keywords, so using keywords in your phrases is a good idea. If, however, your update cannot reasonably fit in the keywords that are relevant to your post, you can always use hashtags as a way to add relevant keywords to your posts. Using hashtags ensures that these keywords can be added without making your update look strange, or like certain words are out of place. For example: "Creating new marketing content today! #digitalmarketer" looks a lot better than "Creating new marketing content today! Digital marketer." When you are using hashtags, do not be afraid to research what popular hashtags exist on Twitter so that you can begin using hashtags that are likely to be trending, thus earning you more traction from your audience.

Once you have begun enforcing all of these strategies on Twitter, you can feel confident that your Twitter page will be optimized for your audience to begin following you and finding what they need from your page. Make sure that you regularly maintain your page by posting updates, updating your cover picture and pinned Tweet, and by keeping your page branded. If you find that your page is not getting as much traction, or that your audience is not aligned with you, you may want to revisit your strategy to ensure that your updates and keywords are relevant to your audience.

Connecting with Fellow Influencers

As with other platforms, getting in touch with fellow influencers is an excellent opportunity to grow on Twitter. When you connect with fellow influencers on Twitter, you can get involved in conversations with them and begin developing friendships with them and growing alongside them. How you do this is important, however, to avoid coming across as ingenuine or pushy. Remember: many people want to become influencers, so if you are not using tact when it comes to growing your account, you are going to find yourself being ignored by influencers and possibly even seen as desperate or inauthentic by potential followers. You want to make sure that you are approaching any influencer you are interested in connecting with using an authentic and sincere approach.

The best way to begin connecting with fellow influencers on Twitter is to discover the influencers that are in your industry and who align with you. Avoid trying to connect with anyone whom you would not normally connect with in real life, as trying to develop relationships with people you are not particularly interested in can be challenging. You do not want to come across as fake in exchange for some likes or followers, as this can compromise your integrity and destroy your ability to grow online. Instead, choose influencers whom you are actually interested in being friends with, as establishing these connections will be much easier.

Once you have identified some influencers that you are interested in, you can begin connecting with them through their profiles. Comment on their content, retweet their posts that you enjoy and otherwise engage with them. Avoid jumping straight into their inbox, as being too forward can make you come across as desperate and needy. Instead, spend some time engaging with their content regularly and showing your support for their content through their comment section and the retweet feature. When the person begins to comment back more, or show reciprocation in your engagement, you can begin moving your friendship into private messages or elsewhere. Building your relationship this way shows that you are not just someone who is trying to get a quick shout out, but instead, are someone who genuinely wants to develop a relationship with this person online.

As you continue to connect with more influencers, realize that the more followers they have, the more time it may take for them to see you and acknowledge you. Do not expect influencers with tens of thousands of followers and hundreds of daily interactions to be able to pick you apart from the crowd right away. In some cases, they may never be able to pick you apart from the crowd as they may be the type of influencer who has grown to the point where they simply cannot keep up with the number of people who are trying to connect with them. If this is the case, be patient and continue connecting anyway. You never know if they may eventually reach out to you and generate a proper connection with you. Even if they don't, staying around people who are doing what you want to be doing is a great way to stay inspired and get yourself out there as you can see new ideas and opportunities arising all the time. Furthermore, people who like the influencer that you also like will begin to see you regularly engaging with them and, as a result, will have an easier time locating and following you.

Researching and Retweeting

When it comes to getting on Twitter, a great tool that you can take advantage of is researching and retweeting other people's posts.

Both of these strategies are an excellent way to stay relevant and get discovered by your audience, so using them regularly is ideal for keeping you active on Twitter and discoverable by your audience. In this section, you are going to learn about what researching and retweeting are and how you can use these two methods effectively.

Researching is a strategy that people use on Twitter so that they can stay up to date on what is trending in the Twitter world. You can use researching as a tool to learn more about your industry, understand what your audience is most interested in that week, and get yourself discovered by people by hopping onto the latest trends. You can also use researching as a tool to identify when trends are dying off so that you can hop off of the trend before you run it into the ground and get seen as irrelevant by your audience. Twitter is one of the best platforms for learning about trends, as it has a discovery tab that is filled with trending topics where you can discover what is trending overall, and what is trending in your preferred areas of interest. You can use this not only to develop trending content for Twitter itself but also to stay trending and relevant on other platforms too.

Retweeting is another great tool that helps you build your content and get discovered. You can retweet Tweets that you find in your research that are relevant to your industry so that you can stay relevant and hop on board with the latest Twitter trends. You can also retweet your favorite influencers as a way to have your account associated with theirs, thus showing your support while also getting yourself seen by a broader audience. Another way to use retweeting as a tool is to retweet your audience or people who regularly show support for you. If your followers post something relevant to your industry, share information about your business, or otherwise share something interesting that your audience would vibe well with, retweeting their tweet is a great way to get seen. You also nurture your relationship with your audience and show that you are interactive and caring, rather than untouchable and distant. This can make your audience feel more connected with you, which increases their chances of staying loyal to you and encouraging their friends and family members to follow you too.

When you are retweeting as a tool, avoid doing it too frequently. While retweeting is definitely a great way to get found and to interact with your audience, it can also lead to you having too many posts on your page that are not curated by you. Having too many retweeted posts can make it seem as though you have nothing to say for yourself, which can make your account have a diluted feel to it. Ideally, you want to be sharing about 70-80% new content, and 20-30% retweeted content. This way, you can share plenty while still having an authentic and personally created voice, making it easier for you to show your brand with your audience.

Growth Hack: Twitter Posting Schedule Sample

One question people often have when it comes to social media, particularly on a platform like Twitter where a conversation is a powerful tool, is: "How often should I be posting?" You want to make sure that you are posting on a consistent basis so that your audience has plenty of content to consume. That being said, you also do not want to feel as though you are spending so much time online that you cannot possibly step away and allow your business to continue growing. You need to ensure that you find a great schedule to post with so that you can keep your account active and growing, without spending too much time online.

The best way to create a posting schedule is to set out a weekly theme schedule, or what you intend to do and post on each day through Twitter. Having a theme for each day and goals for how you will interact online daily can ensure that you are staying focused and that you have plenty to talk about on any given day. You can also curate the weekly theme in a way that keeps your audience fluidly moving through stories so that your audience feels like they are being brought along on a journey with you, rather than just being bombarded with new content that does not seem to flow together.

How you choose to curate your weekly schedule will be up to you, though you should have two elements for your schedule: the themes of each day, and what tasks you want to get done on each day. You should adjust your schedule to include themes that are relevant to your audience to ensure that you are sharing in a way that they receive. Otherwise, below is an excellent sample of how weekly schedules may look for Twitter:

- Monday: #MondayMotivation theme; Talking about what inspires you; 20 minutes engaging with audience; Two pieces of relevant retweeted content

- Tuesday: #TuesdayTips theme; Talking about tips that your audience can use to achieve a certain desired outcome; 20 minutes engaging with audience; Two pieces of relevant retweeted content

- Wednesday: #WednesdayWisdom theme; Talking about a lesson that you have learned that is relevant to your audience; 20 minutes engaging with audience; Two pieces of relevant retweeted content

- Thursday: #ThrowbackThursday theme; Talking about something from the past that is relevant to your audience; 20 minutes engaging with audience; Two pieces of relevant retweeted content

- Friday: #FlexFriday theme; Talking about a rave or something that you are proud of that is relevant to your audience; 20 minutes engaging with audience; Two pieces of relevant retweeted content

- Saturday: #SaturdayVibes theme; Talking about how you are spending the day in a way that is relevant to your audience; 20 minutes engaging with audience; Two pieces of relevant retweeted content

- Sunday: #SelfieSunday theme; Talking about yourself more and introducing yourself to your audience in a relevant way; 20 minutes engaging with audience; Two pieces of relevant retweeted content

By having an easy and consistent schedule for your Twitter experience, it becomes simple for you to know what you need to accomplish every single day to get in front of your audience. Not only will this help you stay on track with your growth, but it also makes it really easy for you to plan out each day's worth of content and upload it. If you wanted to, you could even use a program like Hootsuite or Buffer to prepare your tweets in advance, so that you do not have to do as much on the platform on a day-to-day basis. This way, your content is still being uploaded and seen, and all you have to do is get online for a few minutes per day to retweet a few tweets and share with your audience so that the engagement ratio stays up on your account. This time spent personally engaging will help you build relationships on Twitter as well, making it easier for you to get more followers and build brand relationships and loyalty.

Chapter 6: YouTube Marketing

YouTube is still one of the most powerful platforms in online space, making it an excellent platform for anyone who wants to develop a more personal connection with their audience. YouTube is also great for people who are more interested in connecting with their audience through video since the entire platform is based on video content. Unlike other platforms where you need to regularly comment on people's content and update statuses to stay relevant, YouTube simply requires you to upload videos regularly. Many brands find YouTube to be an excellent avenue for connecting with their audience as it provides them with the opportunity to connect in a more personal manner. Beyond providing an excellent face-to-face connection, YouTube also supplies people with the opportunity to actually *show* their audience something, which makes it easier for their audience to see what they are talking about. Many YouTubers use the platform to show their audience new products, how to videos, or even to teach their audience how their services work so that they can begin getting hired for their services. There are many creative ways to incorporate YouTube into a personal brand or an online small business, which makes it a highly versatile platform.

YouTube functions as a search engine more than a social media account, which means that the way you interact on YouTube is going to be slightly different. Furthermore, you do not necessarily need to spend as much time online with YouTube since most of your content can be created offline, and all you need to do is upload it and then share it so that your content gets seen. For people who prefer to be out living their lives over spending time on social media, getting on YouTube is a great way to build a presence without having to spend quite so much time online.

In this chapter, you are going to discover how you can use YouTube in a way that is relevant in 2019. This way, you can begin building an online presence through this video platform and growing your channel to help you generate the impact that you desire online. Many people make a massive income through YouTube alone, as content creators have many unique opportunities to generate an income in addition to their personal services. For that reason, you may find YouTube to be an excellent primary platform or one to add to your other platforms so that you can have an increased outreach.

Benefits of YouTube

First, let's take a peek at what the many benefits of YouTube are. Many of the benefits have already been outlined above, but there are several more benefits that you can look forward to from getting on YouTube in 2019. One big benefit of YouTube is that it helps you capture the attention of your followers, especially as video content continues to become even more popular than ever before. In 2018, video content rose in popularity to the point that it surpassed most other types of content in regards to what was more likely to turn results. Video content is particularly interesting to people in the modern world because they enjoy watching the content and seeing people in action, and hearing people's voices. Furthermore, YouTube allows you to create content that can be watched or listened to while people are doing other things, which makes it easier for those people to consume your content while they continue doing whatever else they are doing in their life too. This type of passive consumable content also makes it easier for people to include you in their daily lives without having to spend so much time online.

Another great thing about YouTube is that, because it is designed as a search engine, you can keep your content up and have it found for years after your original post. This means that your content lasts much longer and has a better lifespan than content on standard social media accounts. For people who want to be able to post once and have it create ongoing buzz, YouTube is an excellent platform. Many people will make one high-quality video and share it at multiple relevant intervals throughout the future, making it an excellent way for them to draw attention back into deeper parts of their channel.

YouTube is also one of the only platforms that you can use that will truly make a video go viral. Most often, live content or content developed in a native app will not go viral because it is simply not designed in a way that allows it to. On YouTube, however, content can go viral because it is easier for it to be shared around multiple platforms and therefore viewed by multiple users. Many of the videos that go viral online to date are from YouTube, which means that this is your best shot at going viral yourself.

Lastly, getting your YouTube channel up and running can enable you to work YouTube into your other marketing strategies so that you can have an even bigger impact online. For example, YouTube videos can be worked into email marketing campaigns, shared across other platforms, and even offered as freebies to encourage people to opt in to your channel. You can also offer YouTube videos as a part of your private or paid content if you desire to do a video-based membership platform, which is becoming increasingly popular in the online space! Clearly, there are many benefits to YouTube, so getting on YouTube is a great idea to help build your brand if you find that you are the type of person who enjoys filming and sharing video-based content.

Developing Your Channel

YouTube is largely based on sharing videos, so the videos themselves are going to be the biggest way that you generate a buzz around your YouTube channel. That being said, when people find you on YouTube, they are going to want to have an opportunity to learn more about who you are and to decide whether or not you are actually a channel they want to subscribe to. Having a high-quality, well-branded YouTube channel is also a great way to offer a hub for your audience to land on when they find your page so that they can get a feel for who you are. This branded channel can help them find more videos, or even help them find you elsewhere online so that they can become a loyal follower across the Net. Having your YouTube channel properly branded and optimized for your followers is a simple and powerful tool for your audience to benefit from.

To help you effectively develop your YouTube channel, you are going to need to look at your channel as though you were a potential subscriber. A great way to get an idea of what makes a channel great is to look at some of the trending channels out there already and begin getting a feel for how they have been designed and what you think about the designs that have already been created. This is a great way to understand how YouTube branding works and to get a feel for what type of branding you want to employ on your channel.

Once you have gotten a feel for what a branded YouTube account looks like, you can begin by branding yours. First, you want to start your account as a branded business account by creating a channel name that reflects your business. Your channel name can be your personal name, or it can be your brand name. It should match with the professional name that you are using to run your brand, however, so that people know what to look for when they desire to search you up on YouTube. Once you have chosen your channel name, you will also want to choose a channel icon. The icon you choose will also need to be the icon for your Google account, as the two accounts are linked, so make sure that the channel icon you choose is one that you can also use for your Google account—ideally, you should be using either your brand's logo or a professional photo of your face to ensure that you are keeping your brand's identity clear to anyone who may be trying to discover your profile. Lastly, you need to make a header image for your channel, which is often simply called "channel art" on YouTube. Channel art can easily be made on Canva, and all you need to do is design the art so that it reflects your brand. Some people will put their channel name and logo on their channel art, and others will do seasonal themes on their art to keep their channels updated and attractive for their audience.

Once you have updated these basic elements of your page, you want to go through the more in-depth information on your profile. The biggest thing that you want to do here is to go to your "About Me" page and begin filling in information about your business. This is an excellent opportunity for you to give your followers some information about who you are, what you have to offer, and why they should follow you. Although not everyone will read this page, having it available is a great opportunity to give your audience some backstory on who you are and give them the opportunity to follow you elsewhere, or find where they can do business with you if you offer products or services. As with anything, your "About Me" page needs to be informative, interesting and engaging if you are going to be able to effectively get people to read it and then take action on it.

The best way to create an engaging "About Me" page is to be descriptive and to the point. Avoid creating a page that is overwhelming or filled with too much information that is unimportant to your audience, as this will prevent you from having anyone read the page. Instead, stay focused on what is going to be important to your audience, and get to the point quickly within the first two-three sentences. You want to use these sentences to call out your target audience, pitch your channel's value, and describe your channel to the people who are considering following you. This way, people instantly know what you are about and what you have to offer. As you write your page, you should also consider using keywords in a natural manner so that your channel ranks higher with SEO, while still coming across as genuine and impactful.

A great example of an "About Me" page is on Michael Sealy's hypnosis channel:

"Hypnosis – Hypnotherapy – Guided Meditation – Sleep Relaxation

Hi, my name is Michael and welcome to my channel, where I hope you can stop by to relax, listen in, and see for yourself the power of positive hypnosis.

Hypnosis is a completely natural state of often deeply felt relaxation and focused attention, where positive suggestions can be more easily accepted by our subconscious minds. Imagine a fantastic and tranquil state of daydreaming, and that is very close to hypnosis!

Hypnosis can bring us improved self-control, clearer and empowered behavioral choices, and allow us to listen to our best inner resources. Many people experience a deep sense of calmness and serenity during hypnotic meditation and are often pleasantly surprised to see the ongoing, life-enhancing results.

Thank you greatly for your support, feel free to subscribe and comment on your great results, and I trust you will benefit from your time spent with positive hypnosis.

Peace & Enjoy."

This description is well-written in that it is interesting, provides a clear sensory experience for Michael's audience, and creates a clear "call to action", which is to subscribe to his channel, watch his videos, and comment your feedback. Creating these clear call to actions is a great opportunity to encourage anyone who reads your description to begin engaging with your page if they feel drawn into the type of content that you are sharing. If you are an influencer or someone with a business opportunity, you could also include your website or your email address as a part of your call to action so that people can begin doing business with you.

In addition to your "About Me" page, you should also consider the layout of the page itself. Pay attention to certain features like your playlists and community, as these are two valuable tools that you can use to further add to your subscriber's experience. Your playlists can be used to organize your videos based off of popular categories that you film for so that your audience has an easier time finding the content that they are looking for on your page. Playlists are not only a great way for you to create an easier opportunity for your audience to find your videos, but they also help new subscribers get a better feel for everything that you offer to your audience. This way, they can explore your channel and easily discover everything that you have to offer.

Creating Your Aesthetic

In addition to building the structure of your YouTube channel, you also need to begin creating the aesthetic for your YouTube channel. Your aesthetic is essentially the combination of your profile picture, channel art, channel trailer, and the cover photographs that you use for your YouTube page. You want all of these to match so that you can generate an overall image that is on-brand and well designed, which makes it easier for your audience to see what you are all about and instantly decide whether or not they are attracted to your channel.

You have already determined your channel icon and channel art; now it is time for you to begin creating the rest of your channel's aesthetic. Here, you want to begin creating an aesthetic that is going to allow you to generate a uniformed look, but without creating a page that is incredibly boring or uninteresting. If your channel is too uniform, people will think it looks uninteresting because everything looks the same, which can significantly reduce your viewership. You want to have your channel organized with your brand's images in a way that keeps each video looking unique and interesting, while still having similarities. A common tool people will use when they are creating a video's cover image is having the photograph itself change while presenting the channel information and episode title in the same format so that there are similarities on your page. This is a great way for you to create uniqueness and sell each video to your audience, while still keeping a uniformed and branded appearance. You should seek to keep this the same across all of your videos on your entire page unless you are planning on rebranding and designing a new aesthetic.

Your channel trailer is another excellent opportunity for you to brand your page and begin sharing it with your audience. Every single YouTube channel has the space to host a channel trailer, which essentially gives potential subscribers the opportunity to get a feel for who you are, what you have to offer, and why they should begin following you. You want to keep your channel trailer up to date to ensure that the information is relevant and correct and that you are sharing interesting content with your growing audience.

It is important that when you film your channel trailer, you do so with the intention of representing your brand. Your trailer should be under 40 seconds, engaging, interesting, and direct when it comes to telling your audience what to expect when they land on your page. There are many ways that you can film a high-quality trailer, so you are going to need to decide what you desire for your page and what your audience is going to be most receptive to. Ideally, you want to spend those 40 seconds introducing your personality and hooking people into the content on your channel so that they immediately begin to understand what your channel is all about. If you have never seen a YouTube trailer before, you may benefit from looking at similar channels so that you can get a feel for how they have leveraged their channel trailer to support them in gaining more subscribers. This is an excellent opportunity to get an understanding of how you should talk, what you should say, and what specific content should be added to your trailer. For some channels, trailers include an introduction and some talking followed by short clips from other videos, and for others, it is just a clean shot of someone's face as they talk to the camera. You will need to find what aesthetic works best for you based on what you offer your audience and what they are looking for.

The final part of your channel's aesthetic is considering the quality of your videos themselves. When it comes to developing videos for YouTube, creating low-quality content is not going to support you in gaining an audience. You want to make sure that you are creating content that will actually compete with what everyone else is creating. This means that you need to be filming in at least 1080p, although filming in 4K would be preferable since most devices can film and view in 4K these days. You also want to make sure that the content being filmed is of high quality. Avoid filming any content that is being shot in low lighting, with a messy background, or with anything else that may make it sloppy. You want to take your videos seriously so that people take you seriously when they watch your channel. If you are not creating high-quality content, people are going to find that your channel is not as interesting to watch as other people's channels because it lacks a high-quality aesthetic. Instead of watching your content, they will begin to watch the content of those who have taken the time to mindfully create a high-quality background with exceptional lighting and high-quality film.

In addition to getting the original film in higher quality, you can also benefit from learning how to edit your videos so that you can make them even more attractive. Learning about how you can adjust the sound so that it is crisp, how to fix the lighting as needed, and how to add in any headings or text is all important to help you create an even higher quality video. If you are new to film editing, use an easy app like iMovie or Pinnacle Studio. Both software is excellent for helping videographers create higher quality videos for their audience so that their audience can enjoy the film even more. If you are unsure about how to edit films, you can always YouTube simple tutorials to help you get started. Take a look at other professional YouTube channels as well to see how they have edited their content so that you can begin getting an understanding for what high-quality film edits look like, which can also inspire you to edit your content effectively.

Growing Your Channel's Audience

There are many ways that you can grow your channel on YouTube, so you may want to take your time and practice understanding each of these strategies to ensure that you are gaining the fullest growth from your channel possible. At first, using all of these strategies may be intimidating, particularly if you are not used to growing on a search engine platform. As you begin to use them more frequently, these strategies will become easier for you and you will find yourself effortlessly growing so that you can gain even more followers and, as a result, even more potential clients for your brand.

The first thing you want to do when you are in the process of gaining new followers is developing your videos around a single keyword. Because YouTube is a search engine, and search engines thrive off of keywords, choosing and implementing a single keyword can help when it comes to being discoverable by the search engine's algorithm. If you are unsure about what your keyword should be, using a keyword tool like Google Keywords is an effective way to learn about what keywords are relevant to your industry and what people want to know more about. This is not only effective for the SEO (*search engine optimization*) portion of your channel growth, but it can also be used to help you gain inspiration on what type of content you should be filming more of.

It is also important that all of the content you create is high quality, as people want to see high-quality content on YouTube. If you film something and later on decide that the content quality could be higher, do not be afraid to refurbish that content so that you can share an updated version of it. The more you focus on creating higher quality content, including content that looks better and features more interesting information, the better your channel is going to grow. Remember: people are not just watching your videos for nothing; they are watching your videos because they are interesting or because they were captivated by something that you shared. Always look for new ways to increase the quality of your content so that you can regularly improve your channel and keep your audience coming back for more. Just as with other social media platforms, there are always new ways for sharing on YouTube, so staying up to date with the latest trends of the platform and your niche is an excellent way to make sure that you are regularly improving to serve your audience.

Another great way for you to begin developing your channel is by promoting it on other platforms. Getting found on YouTube itself works better if you already have plenty of views and popularity on each video, so do not be afraid to build up other platforms and share your content there to increase the amount of traffic heading to your YouTube channel. If you desire for your YouTube channel to be your main platform, you can always set up a funnel-style feature where all of your other social media platforms will, in one way or another, drive your audience to your YouTube channel. You will learn more about building funnels in Chapter 8.

Lastly, do not be afraid to engage with your audience and make requests of them. Hosting giveaways on your YouTube channel is a great way to encourage people to begin commenting on your videos. You can also encourage comments by simply asking questions in your videos and requesting people leave their preferences in the comments so that you can go through and read them later on. You can also use this same type of dialogue to encourage people to follow your channel or go check out other videos that you have made that they might enjoy. Creating this back-and-forth dialogue with your audience is not only an excellent way to drive them to your channel, but it also creates a more personable and friendly experience for your audience to follow. As well as creating dialogue in your videos themselves, do not be afraid to get into your comment section and start commenting back to your audience when they comment on your videos. This type of connection is a great opportunity for you to begin increasing that back-and-forth dialogue and having even more positive connections with your audience.

In addition to encouraging engagement on your content, do not be afraid to engage on other people's content as well. Remember: YouTube is still considered a form of social media, so increasing your social behaviors on here is a great way to grow. Find channels that resonate well in your industry and that have content you enjoy and do not be afraid to leave comments on their content and engage with them. Not only will this enable you to be seen more, but it can also begin laying the foundation for positive connections from within your industry. For many YouTube channels, this is an excellent opportunity for people to begin collaborating so that they can generate even more success in their YouTube careers. This way, not only do you gain access to your own audience, but you gain access to theirs as well, and they gain mutual benefits from this as well.

Growth Hack: Posting Schedule

One great strategy you can use to grow your YouTube channel is to develop a consistent posting schedule. Think about your channel like a true channel on television: people begin to expect the shows to be uploaded at a certain time, as this gives them the ability to rely on when new content will be made available. This is why people get so invested in shows on television because they know that it will be worth their time since they are interested in the content and they know that there will be more available, and when. The same goes for your YouTube channel: you want to have interesting content that is uploaded on a reliable schedule so that your audience knows *when* to expect new content from you. This schedule should not only be developed for you, but made available to your audience as well so that they know *what* to expect from your channel.

Most major channels will give their audience information about their uploading schedule at the beginning and end of every video, and may even go so far as to include it in their "About Me" page so that their audience knows what to expect. Ideally, you should be aiming to upload one to two new things per week, as this ensures that you have plenty of new content available for your audience to watch. As your channel grows, you will find that not only do you have new content being watched but also that people go back and binge-watch your old content so that they can enjoy the other things that you have made. If you ever want to increase your growth rates, you can always reshare old videos to your other social media accounts to begin getting more traffic going toward them. This also gives your audience the incentive to begin looking at your older content so that they can gain the other valuable information that you have already uploaded to your channel.

As your channel grows, you may find that you need to upload three or four videos per week to keep up—if you really want to accelerate your growth. The more that you upload content, the more your audience will have to consume and enjoy. That being said, make sure that you never increase your posting frequency to something higher than you can reasonably handle, as having anything too high can be overwhelming and may result in you burning out and struggling to keep up your channel growth.

Chapter 7: Blogging for SEO

Blogging is an incredible way to grow in the online space, as it gives you an excellent platform to share with your audience. Unlike other social media platforms where you only share status updates, blogging allows you to go into depth about what you are thinking, or what topic you want to share about. Blogging can be likened to YouTube, except that instead of having videos about the content you want to be sharing you can have longer posts about it. Blogs are an excellent opportunity for you to begin sharing your information, thoughts, and opinions with your audience in a way that is long lasting and easy to consume. Since blogs are archived, you can always dig back into old blog posts to share content with your audience when you find that the content is relevant, which makes being a blogger powerful. The content that you write can always be reused, updated, and shared again which means that everything you write can have lasting value.

When it comes to blogging, there is one very important area of concern that you need to consider when it comes to developing a blog that grows—you do not want to pour all of your energy into developing a blog, only to have no one find it because you failed to consider the search engine optimization element of the blog, also known as SEO. For you to be able effectively to grow your blog and get people locating you, SEO needs to be considered so that you can grow rapidly. You have likely heard of the phrase SEO before, yet you may not know how you can leverage SEO to effectively develop your blog and begin seeing more traffic passing through. In this chapter, we are going to look at the development of a blog as well as the development of blog SEO so that you can hit the ground running, rather than release your posts into a room full of crickets.

Benefits of Blogging

When you use SEO effectively on your blog, the SEO itself becomes one of the biggest benefits of your blog. Blogging with SEO means that your website becomes easier to discover on search engines, which means that you are more likely to have traffic come across your page, which means that in addition to reading your posts, your visitors will also be more likely to find your offerings. This is an excellent opportunity to increase the buzz around your brand and create a more tangible platform for your audience to interact with.

Another great benefit of blogging is that it can be monetized in so many ways. From advertisements and sponsored posts to offering actual products or services on your website, there are many ways that you can leverage a blog to help grow your business. Many people make $1,000+ per month from blogging strictly through advertisements and sponsored posts, making it an excellent choice for developing a passive income online.

If you already have a business developed and are already selling products and services, writing a blog further supports you in becoming an established authority figure in your industry. Ideally, someone who knows enough to write about everything that they know from an expert position can be considered an expert. After all, if you know enough to educate people on a regular basis, you must know plenty to be able to teach and educate people on products or services in your industry too. This gives you credibility and makes it easier for you to begin selling your products and services to your audience, as they can see that you are clearly educated with your industry and that you know enough to guide them through the process of purchasing.

Blogging Platforms You Should Use

There are a few excellent platforms that you can use to help you begin your online blog. These platforms, or website hosts, are platforms that you can use to begin sharing your blog posts with your audience so that you can start growing your actual blog! You want to choose a platform that is going to be cost-effective, easy to navigate, and able to assist you in optimizing your SEO so that you can increase your chances of being discovered on search engines like Google or Yahoo!

If you are looking for a platform that you can completely customize and develop yourself, or have a professional do it for you, WordPress is the best way to go. A WordPress website is an excellent platform that you can use to help you begin your blog as it allows you to customize every single element of your blog using coding like HTML or JavaScript. If you are not familiar with coding, you can always use an easy-to-customize ready-made template to develop your website. Alternatively, you can hire a developer who can support you in developing your WordPress website so that you can simply focus on writing and uploading blog posts to your platform. Depending on what avenue you go with, WordPress can cost anywhere from $100 to $2,500+ to get started. This means that nearly anyone with any budget can get online and develop their blog so that they can start writing a high-quality blog for their followers.

If you are looking for something that you can develop on your own, but do not want to worry about using coding or anything else like that, you can always consider a simpler web host service like Squarespace, Wix, or Weebly. These are click-and-create type websites, where you simply choose a template and then adjust your settings so that your template looks more branded to your personal brand. The benefit of these websites is that you can still have a custom domain name, giving you all of the great benefits of having your own platform to work with. This way, you can have easy web developing software at your fingertips, plus all of the professional benefits of your hosting services.

Other services are available online, such as Medium, although these are not ideal if you are truly looking to generate an income from your blog. Platforms like Medium enable you to contribute to a social media-type platform that allows many contributors to upload blog posts to the platform. Because of how it operates, you will end up having all of your traffic on Medium, rather than on your platform, which can significantly reduce your ability to earn funds through your blog. If you do want to use Medium, you might consider using it as a secondary platform that you can upload blog posts to, and then drive people to your personal blog through these posts. Avoid uploading everything to your Medium account so that you provide people with an incentive to visit your personal blog and begin seeing what you are all about. In this way, you can use Medium like a social media funnel, rather than an actual blog host.

Creating Valuable Content

If you are not creating valuable, high-quality content, you can guarantee that no one is coming to your page. People are not interested in reading regurgitated or uninspired content that they have seen on a thousand other blogs before yours. If you begin creating low-quality content that is filled with unimportant, irrelevant, or outdated information, your followers will start to believe that you are not an expert so much as a follower, which can diminish your credibility. Remember: you outlined why you were so unique earlier in this book for a reason—so that you can sell your uniqueness! Do not be afraid to bring that unique persona into your blog so that people can really get a feel for how and why you are different, while also consuming content that is, at the very least, presented in a new and fresh manner.

Creating valuable content comes down to five different elements: the core topic, the writing itself, the title, the excerpts, and the graphics that you choose to use. You can also use links within your posts to increase the quality of your content, depending on what it is that you are trying to achieve with your audience. By staying mindful of these five elements in every single blog post, you can ensure that you are creating a blog post that is of high quality every single time. Below, we will explore how each of the five posts works together to support you in developing incredible content that your audience will love consuming, sharing, and coming back for.

Core Topic

The core topic that you choose to write about with each blog post needs to be clear and identified before you actually begin to write anything. The more clarity you have around your blog post's topic, the easier it is going to be for you to provide clear, high-quality content for your audience, as you will know where you should keep your focus. You can identify a core topic by considering what is important to your audience at that time, what is trending, and what keywords are presently being searched the most. Narrowing your core topic down to one single keyword is a great opportunity for you to begin with something that is incredibly clear. This also allows you to leverage keywords in your SEO, as SEO thrives on using keywords in content so that search engines can tell whether or not your content is relevant. When you come up with an idea for a topic, use a keyword tool like Google Keywords or Keyword.io to help you identify what keywords are trending around that topic so that you can be very clear on what it is that you will be talking about. If you are using a platform like WordPress to develop your blog, be sure to use an SEO plugin and input your keyword into that plugin so that it can measure how well you are leveraging your SEO on the platform. If not, follow the steps below to ensure that your posts are SEO friendly.

The Writing

The writing itself needs to be of high quality in that you want to avoid having any spelling errors or grammatical errors. Although the odd error may slip through, your content should be fairly clean and professional to ensure that people realize that you are not simply throwing things together and putting them up on the internet to be read. Remember: you want to look like a professional and present your brand professionally, so consider it your job to both write high-quality content *and* edit it effectively too.

When it comes to formatting the content, ideally you should use headers every 300-400 words to ensure that your content is broken up in a way that makes it easier to read. You also want to keep your sentences fairly short, keeping them around 20 words or less, and your paragraphs short, keeping them around three to four sentences in length. Keeping your blog posts in these smaller formats makes them easier to read on mobile devices, which account for a large portion of your readers in many cases. The easier you make your posts to read, the more likely people will be willing to read your content and then return to read more.

When it comes to the SEO side of writing, you want to keep your keyword in use on a fairly consistent basis throughout your post. Ideally, you should mention your keyword enough to account for roughly 2-3% of your overall post, as this ensures that you are mentioning it enough to keep it relevant, but not so much that you overwhelm the SEO into thinking that your post is spammy. This means that you should be mentioning your keyword 30-45 times in a standard 1,500-word blog post, and absolutely no less than 15 times. Remember, when it comes to SEO keywords, you have to use the same variation of the word throughout the post for it to count. So, if your keyword is "cooking" then you must use the word "cooking" to account for 2-3% of your overall word count. "Cook", "cooked", "cooker", and other variations of the word will not count toward your total keyword word count.

The Title

The title that you use for your blog post can be SEO optimized, while also being optimized to capture people's attention so that people are more likely to click the link to your blog post and begin reading it. There are three things that you need to consider when you are creating a title for your blog post: the length of it, the usage of your keyword, and how interesting or engaging the title is. You want to make sure that you are incorporating all three of these elements into your blog post's title to ensure that it is engaging and effectively going to drive your post up higher into SEO results. Ideally, a blog post's title should be around 40 characters long, as this is long enough to provide information about what is in the post, but not so long that it cuts part of the title out of the screen when people are searching for the post. You want to make sure that you use your keyword once in your blog title—preferably toward the beginning of the title, ideally as the very first word in the title. So, if your keyword is "empaths" and you were talking about what types of crystals empaths should be using, you would want your title to be something like "Empaths Need These 5 Crystals!" or something similar. This sample title includes the keyword, an appropriate number of characters and words, and is captivating enough to encourage people to open the post and begin reading what you have written about.

Your Excerpts

Excerpts are often shown on the main page of your blog, or the search page, as well as on social media platforms where you will be sharing your post to encourage people to read it. Ideally, your excerpt should be from your blog post itself so that people can get a feel for what it is that they will be reading from your content. That being said, you should write your posts with the intention of having at least 2-3 sentences of out each post being used as the excerpt for your blog marketing strategies. This excerpt should be interesting, should allude to the content that will be within, and should use your keyword once so that you can have that keyword available on your page. That way, you can use this excerpt all around the net to encourage people to begin reading your blog and paying attention to your posts.

The Graphics

Every single blog should have graphics—ideally ones that are wisely placed to make the blog more appealing to the human eye. For humans, attempting to read too many consecutive words can be stressful, as often they will begin to lose their focus and struggle to read and comprehend everything that was written. Breaking your post up with two-three relevant pictures is a great opportunity for you to make the post more appealing so that people enjoy reading it. These posts can also be designed to share on Pinterest or used to share as the graphics for the social media posts when you are sharing the post itself. This way, they double as a marketing tool for your blog post.

Links (Optional)

When it comes to creating SEO friendly posts, having both internal and external links is a great opportunity to increase the quality of your post and maximize the amount of growth that you get with your page. Ideally, you should be posting at least one internal link and one external link per post, as this guides people around your blog as well as around the internet in general. This type of link sharing leads search engines to believe that you are sharing high-value content that their audience can benefit from, which increases your odds of getting found. You can use internal links to link your audience back to previous posts or to draw them to your services page, and you can use external links to draw them to your social media platforms, to other blogs, or to other resources that you believe they can benefit from.

Posting Frequency Guide

Posting on a blog is something that you need to do consistently to ensure that your audience has plenty of content to consume. Ideally, you should focus on posting at least two-three times per week so that there is plenty of content for your audience to consume regularly. Many bloggers like to have a content calendar that allows them to know which day they will upload on each week so that there is consistency with their strategy. This way, bloggers know when to write and stay consistent, and their audience knows when they can expect new content to come out. That being said, not every blogger will have a specific day of the week that new content will come out. Some bloggers simply aim to upload two-three times per week and then allow themselves to upload organically as the content moves through them.

Ultimately, it is up to you to decide how often you are going to be uploading content to your blog, so you want to choose a schedule that is going to be doable for you. Avoid choosing something that is too overwhelming, as you do not want to overwork your schedule and leave yourself feeling upset that you were unable to keep up with the demands that you placed on yourself. If you are unsure about how much content you can create consistently, consider creating a slower schedule at first and then increasing it as you go, whenever you feel as though you can reasonably handle more demands on your schedule.

Growth Hack: Creating Viral Content

Writing viral blog posts is not the easiest thing to do, but if you can develop a viral blog post, you will find that your overall page grows significantly faster. Viral blog posts are not guaranteed, but there are some steps that you can take to increase the likelihood of your post going viral. First, you should seek to consistently upload content to your blog, as this makes your blog more admirable in the eyes of SEO. The more you upload, the more your blog posts are seen and the more you can increase your chances of being exposed to a viral opportunity through your blog. You want to make sure that you write every single piece of content with the intentions of getting it viral, as this ensures that whichever post does take off is well written, and when people find your blog, they see that all of your content is just as high quality. Make sure that you keep your posts on-trend, too, but avoid making them sound like a copy of what is already out there. Include your authentic voice and approach so that people can see that you are original and generate your own ideas, even if you are writing about something that has already been written about in some capacity. Also decide what type of viral attention you want to have, as this is important to understand before you begin writing a post with the intention of pushing for it to go viral. Some posts go viral because they are shocking or overwhelming, whereas others go viral because they are interesting, inspiring, or positive. Determine what type of attention would be most on-brand for you and write your content with the intention of generating that type of attention through your content, to avoid being recognized as or known for something that is completely off-brand. Finally, make sure that you share all of your content on social media and that you encourage people who read your content to share it too. Social media has a powerful ability to get your content out further, which makes it easier for you to go viral if you often share on social sharing sites. Do not quit trying with every single post you create—the more you create and share, the more likely you are to have a post go viral so that you can really blow up your name and increase your online presence. Even if it takes a while, do not lose hope! You may just be the next *"Cash me ousside, how bow dah?"* or *"Damn, Daniel!"*

Chapter 8: Advertising

Advertising for your brand is imperative if you want to get your name out there and maximize your growth potential. Believe it or not, some of the older advertisement methods are still excellent for developing your brand on social media. In this chapter, we are going to explore three older advertisement methods that still rock on social media: competitions and contests, promo codes, and good old-fashioned sales funnels. If you are ready to really step up your game online, using all three of these is a great way to increase your followers, maximize engagement, and grow your business quickly.

Running Competitions and Contests

A great strategy that was developed years ago, before online businesses even existed, was competitions and contests. These strategies encourage people to begin engaging with your business because it gives them an incentive to win a prize if they do! Online, prizes of all types have been developed and shared with audience members through various competition and contest strategies. You can do anything from encouraging people to comment on and share your posts, to having them upload images with a certain element to them that pertains to your brand. For example, if you are a photography brand, you might have your followers upload their best content and use a specific hashtag or tag your company in it to be entered. This is a great way to get your name out there and increase your brand recognition, while also developing an excellent relationship with your followers.

Using Promo Codes and Special Offers

Promo codes and special offers are another great way to add a layer of incentive to your business, as they allow you to begin giving people an incentive to purchase from you. For people who have never purchased before, promo codes or special offers allow them to feel like they are not spending quite as much money on your products. Therefore, if for some reason they do not like them, they will not feel quite so bad. Of course, you already know that they will love your products or services, so when they fall in love you now have a customer for life and, ideally, you make your discounted price back plus plenty more. If you have people who have purchased in the past but who have not made a purchase in a while, promo codes and special offers provide them with an incentive to purchase your products again.

If you want to really dig deeper into the world of promo codes, you can also start working together with influencers in your industry who may be willing to test your products or services and share them with their audience. After these individuals have tried your products or services, you can give them a promo code to share with their audience so that their audience can begin purchasing your products or services too. In order for this to work, you will also need to be willing to offer your influencers some form of commission or incentive to share. This way, they are also benefiting from sharing your brand with their audience, so it is a win-win situation.

Creating Sales Funnels

Sales funnels are a powerful tool to use when it comes to developing your business online too. Sales funnels are tools that you use to drive your audience around your online presence, often to get them to your sales page so that they can purchase your products or services. To develop a sales funnel, you first need to decide what you want your audience to do, as this will help you determine where you need to be sending them to. A common example of a sales funnel is as follows:

1. Your audience starts by finding you and following you on social media

2. From social media, your audience is led to your website, where they can sign up for your free offer and subscribe to your email list

3. From their free offer, they are guided to your low-end offer, often called a trip wire, which encourages them to buy something inexpensive from you

4. If they enjoy their inexpensive product from you, your audience is often then encouraged to purchase something of higher value from you

5. Finally, if they liked that offer, they can purchase your highest end value

At the end of the day, your sales funnel is intended to get people from being your followers on social media to purchasing your best offers online. This way, you can monetize your followers and generate a consistent income online, thus making it easier for you to begin really leveraging your social media marketing for profitable growth.

Conclusion

Congratulations on completing *Social Media Marketing: Unlock the Secrets of Personal Branding to Grow Your Small Business and Become an Influencer Using YouTube, Facebook, Instagram, Blogging for SEO, Twitter, and Advertising!*

This book should have helped you to have a positive understanding of how social media can be leveraged to support you in growing your online business. Growing your online business through social media is a powerful opportunity for you to access a larger segment of your target audience so that you can really scale your business, and fast. When you use your social media platform to grow your business, not only do you increase your capacity for growth, but you also increase your capacity to develop the ability to engage in a freedom-based lifestyle. If you choose to, you can leverage your personal brand and online income to support you in living a freedom-based lifestyle so that you can travel, take days off, and enjoy life as you please all while still making a consistent income.

The next step after reading this book is to begin developing your online brand. Choose two-three platforms that you want to develop on, and begin developing your brand through these platforms based on the steps provided for you within this book. The more you work toward developing these platforms, the easier it will be for you to keep growing your platform and developing a larger audience. Remember that each platform will have its own learning curve, so if you find yourself struggling to create results right away, take your time and remain consistent while regularly reviewing your approach. In time, you will discover how you can easily maintain your online platforms without having to put quite so much work into understanding how they work and what types of strategies increase your ability to get discovered.

Lastly, if you enjoyed this book and feel that it was valuable in supporting you with growing your brand on social media, please consider leaving a review on Amazon Kindle. Your honest feedback would be greatly appreciated.

Thank you, and good luck!

Check out another book by Matt Golden